The Allied landings that took place in Southern France in August 1944 represented both one of the concluding elements of the wartime Mediterranean campaign and a decisive follow-on to the invasion of Normandy that had taken place two months before. It was viewed by many at the time as something of a sideshow and not a significant part of the wider war effort. Considerable controversy surrounded the planning of what was originally known as Anvil with the senior Allied political and military leaders heatedly debating the strategic rationale for such an operation. The maritime force of escort carriers, a gun support force, minesweepers, cargo vessels and heavy landing craft was commanded by an American admiral but a third of it was supplied by the Royal Navy. On the day of the landings the British cruiser HMS *Argonaut* fired the most rounds of any ship in the fleet. An overwhelming superiority in airpower and a lack of a cohesive German response meant that the landings were an overwhelming success. By the third day the Allies held a 50-mile front as much as 30 miles deep, a total of some 500 square miles. At least nine important towns were in Allied hands and spearheads were ten miles from the naval base of Toulon, ten miles from Cannes. Seaborne and airborne troops had met ashore and reinforcements and supplies were being landed in large quantities. As this Naval Staff History highlights even so "The Champagne Campaign", as it was later termed by many of those who had been involved, required considerable planning and the contribution provided by the Royal Navy had a significant part to in the final Allied success. With this came the capture of intact French ports and the establishment of a vital logistic hub would help safeguard the Allied drive through North-Western Europe.

This is the second volume in Helion's new series, 'Naval Staff Histories of the Second World War'. The series aims to make available to a broad readership these indispensable studies of the key operations of the war.

Naval Staff Histories of the Second World War

1. *Operation Neptune: The D-Day Landings, 6 June 1944*, edited by Tim Benbow (ISBN 978-1-909982-97-0)
2. *Operation Dragoon: The Invasion of the South of France, 15 August 1944*, edited by Andrew Stewart (ISBN 978-1-909982-98-7)

DR ANDREW STEWART FHEA, FRHistS

Dr. Andrew Stewart is currently the Director of Academic Studies (KCL) at the Royal College of Defence Studies based in London. He has been a member of the Defence Studies Department, King's College London, the academic component of the United Kingdom's Joint Services Command and Staff College, since 2002 and has previously served as the Assistant Dean of Academic Studies and the Land Historian supporting the Higher Command and Staff Course. In 2014 the title of 'Reader in Conflict and Diplomacy' was conferred upon him.

The focus of his research relates to the Second World War and he has produced three sole-authored books, *Empire Lost: Britain, the Dominions and the Second World War* (2008), *A Very British Experience: Coalition, Defence and Strategy in the Second World War* (2012) and, most recently, *Caen Controversy: The Battle for Sword Beach 1944* (2014). In addition he has edited a number of co-authored volumes and written various articles for leading academic journals. He remains a committed military historian and is currently working on his next two books, one examining the East African campaign and the other British home defence planning through the wartime years. He is Co-Director of the King's Second World War Research Group.

He is married to Joanne, who works for the UK's Ministry of Defence, and lives in Oxford.

Naval Staff Histories of the Second World War Volume 2

OPERATION DRAGOON

The Invasion of the South of France, 15 August 1944

Edited by

Andrew Stewart

Helion & Company

Helion & Company Limited
26 Willow Road
Solihull
West Midlands
B91 1UE
England
Tel. 0121 705 3393
Fax 0121 711 4075
Email: info@helion.co.uk
Website: www.helion.co.uk
Twitter: @helionbooks
Visit our blog http://blog.helion.co.uk/

Published by Helion & Company 2015
Designed and typeset by Battlefield Design, Gloucester (www.battlefield-design.co.uk)
Cover designed by Paul Hewitt, Battlefield Design, Gloucester (www.battlefield-design.co.uk)
Printed by Lightning Source Ltd, Milton Keynes, Buckinghamshire

Text and maps originally appeared as Tactical and Staff Duties Division, (Historical Section), Naval Staff, Admiralty, Battle Summary No.43, "Invasion of the South of France : Operation "Dragoon", 15th August, 1944".

Cover: 'Landing craft approach the French coast, 15 August 1944' (NARA)

ISBN 978-1-909982-98-7

British Library Cataloguing-in-Publication Data.
A catalogue record for this book is available from the British Library.

For details of other military history titles published by Helion & Company Limited contact the above address, or visit our website: http://www.helion.co.uk.

We always welcome receiving book proposals from prospective authors.

Contents

III—The Follow Up

Appendices

Index

List of Plans

(at end of book)

Operation Dragoon: New Introduction

"Anvil will be launched at the earliest possible date. You will use every effort to meet a target date of 1 August. You will prepare for the operation on the basis of approximately a 3 division assault, an airborne lift for the equivalent of 1 division and a build-up to at least 10 divisions as quickly as the resources made available to you will permit, having in mind in your preparations the steady reduction in German capacity to resist and the vital importance of prompt support of the Overlord operation".[1]

Operation Dragoon, or more accurately Operation Anvil as it was termed until very late in the planning process, is perhaps most often recalled as a prominent example of disagreement and discontent amongst the principal Allied political and military leaders about the alliance's grand strategy. Indeed, almost from the outset, there were considerable tensions about both its purpose and aims. For the United States it was a vital strand of the European campaign, bringing additional pressure to bear on German forces and providing a means of allowing French troops to join the battle to liberate their own country. Once the invasion of France had begun with the Normandy landings in June 1944, perhaps the most important consideration became the access to ports that Anvil potentially offered, through which manpower and equipment could be landed to sustain the drive onwards into Germany. There was never, however, any similar enthusiasm from the British who viewed the proposed invasion of Southern France as a distraction from the campaign in Italy, which could lessen the chances for any speedy defeat of the Axis in Europe. Irrespective of the merits of either side of this debate, the assessment of one military historian that it "may have been the most underrated amphibious campaign of World War II" is difficult to refute.[2] For a variety of reasons the large task force that assaulted beaches along the Côte d'Azur on 15 August 1944 achieved a rapid and decisive victory. This introduction aims to provide some background and context, to elaborate on a few key issues and offer a conclusion about the operation's contribution to the wider campaign, closing with some suggestions for further reading.

The Allied Wartime Strategy

The possibility of launching an invasion of Southern France was first raised seriously at the Quadrant conference held in Quebec in August 1943 when it was discussed as part of the range of actions that would be conducted to draw German divisions away from France prior to the Normandy invasion. In October a report was then produced which was co-authored by General Dwight D. Eisenhower, at the time Allied Commander-in-Chief Mediterranean, and General Sir Frederick Morgan who, in his role of 'Chief of Staff

1 The National Archives, Kew (hereafter 'TNA'): CAB 122/1246, British Joint Staff Mission (Washington, DC) to COS, 27 June 1944.

2 Clarke, Jeffrey J., 'The Champagne Campaign', *Military History Quarterly* (Vol.20 No.2; Winter 2008), p.37; Roskill, Captain S.W.in his official history, *The War at Sea: Vol.III, The Offensive, Part II, 1st June 1944 – 14th August 1944* (London: Her Majesty's Stationery Office, 1961), pp.104-106.

to the Supreme Allied Commander (Designate)', a long title that was more commonly referred to by its 'COSSAC' acronym, had been given overall responsibility for producing an initial plan for how Europe would be invaded. This document concluded that if Operation Overlord (the campaign to liberate North-West Europe) was judged to have been successful, a diversionary attack could be directed against the port of Toulon. There were, however, a number of caveats, notably resulting from a shortage of landing craft, which limited the assault to a single division. Despite planning for an invasion of Europe having started in late 1941, transport for amphibious operations was extremely limited and this critical shortage would ultimately have a large part to play in helping create huge political and strategic tensions.[3] There was also some more general discussion even at this initial stage about whether there might be a better use of resources, such as an attack further east drawing German troops towards southern Germany or the Balkans, and it was clear that support was muted. The reference to other possible areas of focus was significant and would remain a constant feature throughout the entire planning phase. At the Sextant conference held in Tehran in November 1943, Britain's Prime Minister Winston Churchill led his Chiefs of Staff in advocating the merits of expanding operations in Italy. Nonetheless agreement followed that what was initially referred to as Operation Anvil would be one of the two key operations in 1944 – the other being Overlord – and that it should as far as possible entail a two division assault.

From this stage forward British and American thinking followed increasingly divergent paths. With Eisenhower's appointment as Supreme Allied Commander responsible for the Normandy landings confirmed by the end of 1943, he now became much more enthusiastic about an attack on Southern France. At the same time British planners grew less convinced of its merits and argued that trying to conduct both landings would result in 'skimping' and have the potential for weakening them both fatally. General Sir Bernard Montgomery had been appointed Commander-in-Chief 21st Army Group on Christmas Day 1943, making him Overlord's Commander-in-Chief Land Forces. He advised Churchill at the beginning of January 1944 that Anvil would have no direct positive impact on operations in Normandy for at least 90 days, further undermining any potential for the development of British support. With the debate reaching its conclusion about the final size and date for the assault phase of Overlord, Eisenhower remained convinced that both proposed landings needed to be viewed as one; even with only a potential single division offering more a 'threat' than a tangible fighting force, he was adamant that Anvil should be retained. Further complicating the situation, in February the campaign in Italy, which only the month before had seemed to be progressing well, now suffered a serious check when the Germans counter-attacked against the Anzio beachhead.[4] Indeed it quickly became apparent that the Gustav Line would be defended

3 Stewart, Andrew, *Caen Controversy: The Battle for Sword Beach 1944* (Solihull: Helion and Company, 2014), pp.11-22; TNA: CAB106/1117, 'The Anvil Debate', AL.3011/8.C, pp.1-5.

4 There are two excellent narrative sources detailing the Italian campaign. The first is the official account by Field Marshal the Viscount Alexander of Tunis, 'Despatch on operations of the Allied Armies 1943 Sept. 3-1944 Dec. 12', 12 June 1950, No.38937, which can be downloaded from the excellent 'Hyperwar' online resource http://www.ibiblio.org/hyperwar/UN/UK/londongazette.html. The other is the three relevant volumes from the British official history of the Mediterranean campaign, sections of which can also be found online: Molony, C.J.C, *The Mediterranean and Middle East, Volume V: The Campaign in Sicily, 1943 and the Campaign in Italy, 3rd September 1943 to 31st March 1944* (London: Her Majesty's Stationery Office, 1973); Molony, C.J.C, *The Mediterranean and Middle East, Volume VI, Part I: Victory in the Mediterranean: 1st April to 4th June 1944* (London: HMSO, 1984); General Sir William Jackson with Gleave, Group Captain T.P., *The Mediterranean and Middle East, Volume VI, Part II: Victory in the Mediterranean: June to October 1944* (London: HMSO, 1987).

at all costs, as would be most famously demonstrated with the battles at Monte Cassino, making the advance to Rome a slow and often desperate business.[5] Allied grand strategy was in danger of becoming overloaded.

An often difficult debate followed throughout the next two months with the US Joint Chiefs of Staff adopting the same line as Eisenhower in their demands that the operation should take place. In the American assessment, Anvil continued to have huge potential benefits. In the first instance it was seen as the most obvious way to introduce French troops onto the continent; with their main troop base in Northern Africa and Italy, and having very little involvement in Overlord, they had been given a key role in the landings on what was their southern coast. The capture of the important ports of Toulon and Marseilles also offered huge potential logistic advantages to the Allies and could help ease the unavoidable supply problems that had been recognised within the Overlord plan. A potentially decisive intervention came on 20 March with an appreciation produced by General Sir Maitland Wilson, the senior British officer who had taken over Eisenhower's Mediterranean command. This outlined the situation he believed existed in his theatre and, whilst it acknowledged that the prospects in Italy had improved, it also concluded that the German defences remained unbroken. Wilson expected to capture the vitally important city of Rome before 15 June but he cautioned about the removal of any forces until then as this might potentially hinder his success. He also warned that Anvil would quickly be recognised by the Germans as having only limited objectives and instead of drawing their reserves south, as the American planners anticipated, the defenders could instead potentially seal off the bridgehead in the Rhône Valley and withdraw forces further north to Normandy.[6] As such, he recommended the operation in Southern France be cancelled and asked that all available forces should instead be concentrated on the Italian front.

Despite his earlier comments, three days later Eisenhower also produced a memorandum which broadly agreed with Wilson and largely dismissed Anvil on the grounds that the time did not exist to make adequate preparations. He instead urged that there should be quick progress in northern Italy and asked for the transfer of landing craft to support Overlord. This might have appeared to be a potentially critical interjection but the American Chiefs did not concur and would not back down from their support for the Southern France proposal. They offered a single concession, the launch date being put back to mid-July, and also agreed to switch landing craft from the Pacific to the Mediterranean, but nothing more. In turn their British equivalents now determined that they could not commit to the new date for the invasion and relations between the two sides deteriorated. So much so that the situation remained uncertain until 19 April, when the Chief of the Imperial General Staff, General Sir Alan Brooke, wrote in his diary, "At last our troubles about Anvil … are over. We have got the Americans to agree, but have lost the additional landing craft they were prepared to provide. History will never forgive them for bargaining equipment against strategy and for trying to blackmail us into agreeing with them by holding the pistol of withdrawing craft at our heads".[7] There had been some hard bargaining as a result of which the Mediterranean front seemed to

5 Ibid., pp.10-11.
6 Ibid., pp.14-15.
7 Diary Entry, 19 April 1944 in Danchev, Alex and Todman, Daniel (eds.), *War Diaries 1939-1945 – Field Marshal Lord Alanbrooke* (London: Phoenix Press, 2002), p.541.

have been potentially weakened. Wilson now received a directive informing him that Anvil was, once again, to be considered only as a 'threat' and it was left to him to use the proposed one-divisional assault lift as effectively as he could.[8]

By the beginning of May 1944 there were four possibilities being considered by the British general. Two of these were referred to in generic terms and indicated landings in a particular part of France. The first was still Anvil but in addition there was a favourite alternative project of Churchill named Caliph. For the British leader this entailed a coup-de-main operation involving approximately 50,000 troops who would capture a port on the western coast of the country. This was most likely Bordeaux and its seizure had an obvious appeal in that it was much closer to where the anticipated main battle would be taking place in Normandy than any operation that might successfully result in the capture of Toulon. Some 50 miles up the River Gironde, this assault would, however, be a hazardous undertaking with no guarantee of success. Wilson's two other options were for a landing on the Genoese coast behind the German lines – which was reportedly his favourite – or on the eastern shores of the Adriatic.[9] In each case the scope and timing was to depend upon the progress being made with Overlord. There was also confirmation that the first two plans were only to be conducted if there were clear signs that the defending forces were on the verge of collapse, and all of them depended on a German withdrawal from their current defensive positions in Italy.

It was at this point that the landing craft issue returned. On being briefed about Wilson's proposals, the American Chiefs of Staff reversed their earlier objections and indicated that they would now after all send 19 of the large Landing Ship, Tank (LST) craft to the Mediterranean and these would arrive at some stage in late June or early July.[10] Production of LSTs and other landing ships and craft in the United States had been late in getting under way; large numbers were only being constructed by the winter of 1942-43 before then rapidly falling off again. The repercussions of the production decisions taken earlier in the conflict were felt during 1943 and 1944 until Churchill at last complained with some bitterness that: "the destinies of two great empires… seemed to be tied up in some god-dammed things called LSTs whose engines themselves had to be tickled on by … LST engine experts of which there was a great shortage".[11] A total of 1,051 would be built during the war, almost all in the United States, but fewer than 300 were in existence in November 1943 and of these, 139 were in the Mediterranean. Except for a small contingent, these were all earmarked for the transport of British forces in the planned Neptune landings as soon as the amphibious phases of the Italian campaign were completed. There was an agreement that an additional 62 new LSTs would be provided for the Normandy operation but the remaining new production was allocated to the war in the Pacific. American commanders in this theatre were in direct competition for this critically important component of amphibious operations and this was a major factor in stoking the tensions at the most senior leadership levels.

Throughout May discussions continued about the various alternative plans in the Mediterranean but Allied successes immediately prior to the launch of the invasion of

8 TNA: CAB106/1117, 'The Anvil Debate', pp.18-19.
9 Stanton, W.I., 'Could WW2 Have Ended in 1944: Was Anvil a Big Mistake?', *Army Quarterly and Defense Journal* (No.122; July 1992), pp.347-359.
10 TNA: CAB106/1117, 'The Anvil Debate', p.20.
11 Harrison, Gordon A., *Cross Channel Attack* (Washington DC: Center of Military History, United States Army, 1989), p.64.

France precipitated the final, and most serious, dispute about future strategy. Rome fell on 4 June and as a result, the British repeated much more forcefully their argument warning that Anvil ran the risk of throwing away what had been achieved in Italy. The Chiefs of Staff in London now advised Churchill that troops should not be prematurely withdrawn, while General Sir Harold Alexander, commanding the 15th Army Group, put forward bold proposals to try and push further north in Italy as quickly as possible, potentially seizing Turin and Genoa to create bases for operations in Austria and Yugoslavia. Yet around the same time, on 7 June, Wilson stepped back from his earlier concerns and reported that in light of recent events he could now definitely commit to Anvil and fixed 15 August as the target date; two British generals had reached very different conclusions about what should happen next.

Once again the various planning staffs embarked upon a period of strategic reflection as each of the options that had first been mooted earlier in the year was minutely reconsidered. The difference was, however, that by this stage Neptune had been conducted and the battle for Normandy was now well underway.[12] As such, Eisenhower was even more strongly in favour of some form of assault against Southern France, not least because he was worried about failing to capture enough ports to sustain his advance. There was also some concern about the degree to which the retreating Germans could easily demolish the railways and transport networks from Brest to the Metz region; both would have a significant impact on his ability to develop Overlord and prosecute the campaign to a successful conclusion. There also remained a concern that his right flank would be vulnerable if adequate provisions were not made to clear out the rest of occupied France, as well as there being a requirement to find a role for the free French forces. To the Supreme Allied Commander, Anvil overcame all of these problems.

On 25 June Eisenhower sent a telegram to the Combined Chiefs of Staff urging that the various other projects that had been proposed during recent months should now no longer be considered. He argued that none of them could be launched in time to assist him in Northern France and explicitly rejected the idea that any advance to Trieste, as part of Alexander's proposed drive through to the Ljubljana Gap, would divert significant numbers of German forces. He also reiterated that Anvil should take place on the proposed target date and asked that, if it had not been launched within two weeks, the landing craft that had been assigned were to be instead made available to support Overlord. Throughout the last week of June "an intense argument raged between the British and the Americans – both sides themselves unanimous and sincerely convinced of the importance and logic of their respective theses".[13] It was during this period that Churchill issued his famous warning about "a forlorn march up the Rhône Valley", which he condemned as a potentially "bleak and sterile" move, as he corresponded directly with the American leader, President Franklin Roosevelt, urging upon him the merits of an attack towards Trieste.

This effort proved wasted and on 30 June, with advice from his Chiefs of Staff who warned him "further discussion is useless", the British leader reluctantly agreed to Eisenhower's approach. With troops being withdrawn from the Italian campaign,

12 Benbow, Tim, *Operation Neptune: The D-Day Landings, 6 June 1944* (Naval Staff Histories of the Second World War) (Solihull: Helion and Company, 2015).

13 TNA: CAB106/1117, 'The Anvil Debate', p.24.

Alexander wrote that "the ghost of Anvil hangs heavily over the battlefield".[14] Churchill had agreed reluctantly but the British leader was clearly angered by the course of action that had been forced upon him. He wrote to his confidant and South African counterpart Jan Smuts the following week complaining that "major hopes in Italy" had been "ruined by an American insistence on concentrating on a minor project".[15] The following day, 6 July, he again complained to General Sir Hastings Ismay, the senior British officer who acted as his personal liaison to his Chiefs of Staff, that the landing craft had been "stolen [for the] tomfoolery of Anvil" and they would be found "sprawling in the suburbs of Marseilles".[16] It was in this same letter that he even proposed that there should in future be two commands in the Mediterranean, the Americans "playing the fool at Anvil" with Britain "doing the best it can towards Trieste", but he was persuaded that this should not be issued. Throughout July he continued to agitate against the operation and it fell to those around him to prevent any one of a number of similar "trenchant and vehement telegrams" that he had drafted from being sent. One that did go complained to President Roosevelt about his one-sided control of events and pressed for greater consideration; arguing that all possible forces in the Mediterranean should be sent to Italy, Churchill bitterly described the British as "ill-treated and furious".[17] The war correspondent Chester Wilmot concluded that the American forces he encountered throughout the war were "militarily unsophisticated" but, accurate or not, after their experiences at the Casablanca conference in January 1943, they had quickly become extremely adept at imposing their political will.[18]

Prompted by his senior military advisers, for security reasons Churchill also agreed that the name of the operation should be changed and the significance of the new name, Dragoon, was subsequently noted.[19] There was also one last opportunity to try and divert forces elsewhere as the success of Operation Cobra, launched by American forces in the last week of July from positions just south of the city of St Lô, quickly suggested that the long anticipated breakout in Normandy had begun. The response from the British leader was to propose that his cherished Operation Caliph could be used to open up the Brittany ports, allowing the forces earmarked for the southern landings to be fed much more quickly into the main battle. Although he was supported by his senior military comrades in London, the initial loading of forces destined for Anvil had begun and Eisenhower could not be persuaded otherwise. Southern France would be invaded.

Planning the Invasion of Southern France

Churchill's final, almost desperate attempts to stop Dragoon ignored the fact that detailed planning for how such an operation might be conducted had been going on for many months. This had begun at the Allied Forces' Headquarters at Caserta near Naples in late 1943 and, despite the arguments being made by the senior commanders, had quickly calculated that an approximately three divisional lift would be needed. This would, in turn, build-up to a force of ten divisions – only two of which would be

14 TNA: PREM3/271/8, COS to Churchill, 30 June 1944; CAB106/1117, 'The Anvil Debate', p.26.
15 TNA: PREM3/271/5, Churchill to Smuts, 5 July 1944.
16 TNA: PREM3/271/9, Churchill to Ismay, 6 July 1944.
17 Edmonds, Robin, *The Big Three: Churchill, Roosevelt and Stalin in Peace and War* (London: Penguin Books, 1992), pp.372-376.
18 Wilmot, Chester, *The Struggle for Europe* (London: Collins, 1952), p.128.
19 Churchill, Winston, *The Second World War* (London: Penguin Books, 1989), p.800; Roskill, *The War at Sea 1939-1945: Volume III, Part II*, pp.85-86.

armoured, due to the unsuitable terrain – which it was anticipated would, following its successful landing, exploit inland up to a distance of 225 miles.[20] The initial assessment highlighted that approximately two-thirds of this force should be French; in order to simplify administration and organisation, it was also determined that British formations would play only a limited part and would instead focus on continuing the battle in Italy. The planners in the G-3 Section also reached an early conclusion that the landings should take place to the east of Marseilles where the country, while very mountainous, benefitted from good roads and railways although it was also noted that to the west it was "strongly canalised and numerous defiles between hills and lagoons exist".[21] The early capture of a port was essential and of the three that were in the region – the other two being Toulon and Sète – Marseilles was by far the best. The modified planning report issued in January 1944 stipulated that the primary goal of what was still referred to at this initial stage as the 'Mediterranean diversion' was to prevent the Germans from withdrawing forces from Southern France during the opening phase of Overlord. The target date remained the beginning of May but the size of the opening attack had been reduced to one assault division, to be followed by eight more. Once ashore the Allied force was to move northwards towards Lyon and Vichy, a distance of about 225 miles. It was notable that even from the outset there was some clear recognition of the potential limitations of this exercise. According to the chief Allied planner: "I consider that more German divisions are likely to be contained in Southern France by the mounting of a threat on as large a scale as possible than by the actual launching of an operation which, after the first 48 hours, will have displayed its weakness".[22] It was also still stressed that the assault was not to commence before the attack in Normandy.

Most of the detailed planning had been conducted by the staff of the US Seventh Army in Italy, working under the cover designation of 'Force 163'. The Army group commander had until March 1944 been Lieutenant General George Patton but when he departed for England, and with his nominated replacement Lieutenant General Mark Clark still leading the Fifth Army in Italy, Major General Alexander Patch took charge. He had previously led the United States' XIV Corps which had pushed the Japanese off Guadalcanal, and was one of a very small group of senior US Army officers who commanded troops in both theatres. In early spring 1944 the planners were joined by French staff officers who shared their knowledge of the French Provençal coast. In the first instance, the planners were looking for a landing area which combined an adequate extent of beaches, closeness to a suitable port, the possibility of the seizure of an airfield and comparatively good terrain for the deployment of troops. In many respects this was once again similar to the parameters that had been adopted by the COSSAC team in their earliest reviews of possible targets for the Neptune landings. As one of the senior planners in Naples commented, "Relatively few knew they were going to invade France, though many may have suspected it. Knowledge of the target area was limited to senior commanders, staff officers and key enlisted men whose duties required them to know the plan at the time. Secrecy was vital".[23] At the same time, for some weeks it was widely

20 TNA: WO204/1475, 'Anvil Presentation – 27 December 1943'.

21 Ibid.

22 Ibid., 'Operation Anvil (Modified)', 20 January 1944.

23 Jenkins, Brigadier-General Reuben E., 'Operation "Dragoon" – Planning and Landing Phase', *Military Review* (August 1946), p.4.

believed in the G-3 Section that the entire process was destined to become little more than a 'Command Post Exercise'.[24]

Early in the process four alternative areas along the French coast had been identified as offering the best prospects for a successful landing. The first were the beaches directly south of Marseilles, although it was also recognised that coast defences in this area were the heaviest of any in Southern France. The areas around Rades de Bormes to Cap Camarat had much lighter defences but were up to 100 miles from Toulon and Marseilles, and there were no existing airfields or ports. Fréjus to Saint-Raphaël was further away but had lighter defences along with the benefits of an airfield and a port. Finally there was Cannes and Nice where there were ports with greater capacity, 600 and 2,500 tons respectively, with the added advantage of a natural defensive flank in the form of the Alps, which would considerably reduce the extent of the bridgehead needing to be defended. The Nice area was also farther away from the estimated assembly area of the German mobile reserves, making their arrival at the potential landing beaches later than it would be elsewhere. A fairly straight-forward process of deduction reduced the planners' focus to the last two alternatives and, despite the concerns that the landings might be 'bottled up', it was nonetheless decided that, providing the attacking Allied forces in Italy were north of the Pisa-Rimini line, the assault would be made around the Nice area. Failing that there would be a wait until the Marseilles area defences were reduced sufficiently for a direct landing to be made there.

With the key decision taken, more detailed study and preparation could take place, in large part repeating the process that had been followed by the Neptune team. The terrain in the target area consisted of a rugged and irregular coastline and most of the beaches were relatively short; there were, however, 16 individual beaches that varied from 500 to 4,500 yards long and 10-50 yards wide. Behind most of the beaches there was a narrow belt of sand dunes, some of which were covered with small scrub trees. Inland from the dunes were wooded slopes, cultivated fields, marshy soft sand areas, small streams, farm roads, scattered farm houses and villages. There was a small narrow tarmacadam 'scenic' road running along the coast and a main east-west road from Toulon to Cannes, three to five miles inland apart for the 10-mile stretch from Sainte-Maxime to Fréjus where it joined the coastal road. North of the main road lay the Massif des Maures, a hill mass about 35 miles long by 10 miles wide and 1,000-1,500 feet high. Further to the north there was the Argens River valley and north of that the steeper Alpes de Provence.

On 2 July General Wilson issued a directive confirming that Anvil was to be launched at the earliest possible date, with the target remaining 15 August. It was a truly multinational force that was assembled for the operation. The United States' VI Corps was to conduct the assault phase, drawing upon three infantry divisions commanded by Major General Lucian K. Truscott and known as 'Kodak Force'. This force would land a division on both the western and northern beaches of the Rade d'Hyères, with a third division landing at either side of the Cap Benat. Those troops landing on the western beaches were also to capture the airfield at Hyères. Each Regimental Combat Team would be supported by 10-15 tanks from the French 5th Armoured Division, 'Sudre Armoured Combat Command', under Brigadier General Aime Sudre, which was to provide immediate reinforcements.

24 Weiss, Steve, 'The Invasion of Southern France: Operation ANVIL-DRAGOON, August 1944', in Lovering, Lieutenant Commander T.T.A., RN (ed.), *Amphibious Assault: Manoeuvre from the Sea, Amphibious Operations for the Last Century* (Woodbridge: Seafarer Books, 2007), p.346.

The actual assault areas were designated as 'Alpha Beach' on the left with 3rd Infantry Division landing around Cavalaire-sur-Mer, the 45th Infantry Division in the centre at 'Delta Beach' near Saint-Tropez, and 36th Infantry Division on the right at 'Camel Beach' around Saint-Raphaël. The experience of Normandy had confirmed that the planners' concerns about the amount of fighting power needed for the assault phase were well founded. Nonetheless, because of the terrain, the initial attack had to be restricted to a three divisional front in order to avoid a cramped bridgehead and allow the necessary maintenance troops and stores to be properly deployed.

Having destroyed all immediate enemy opposition, the next mission for Kodak Force would be to prevent all German troop movements between Marseilles and Cavalière and then, more broadly, to hamper their activities within 200 miles of the coast. Finally there was also a requirement to assist if possible in containing the maximum possible number of enemy troops in northern Italy.[25] It was hoped that by one day after the landing, D+1, the beachhead would be extended to a depth of 14 miles. Following up the initial assault, and to be landed by no later than D+2, would be the French II Corps led by General Jean de Lattre de Tassigny, which would eventually include five infantry and two armoured divisions and be re-designated as an army group.[26] Their role was critical, as if the Germans did counter-attack it would be down to the follow-up waves of troops to halt them. According to the French commander, his force was "a living representation of the whole empire … bringing freedom to the homeland and restoring it to its place in the world"; one Algerian and two Moroccan divisions, along with the corps headquarters, were earmarked to provide the initial French component.[27] 'Garbo Force', as it was referred to, was to land in the St Tropez-Cavalaire region, pass through the west side of VI Corps and eventually capture Toulon; with this done they were to continue to attack and seize Marseilles. According to the planners' timeline, by D+9 the aim was for a total of four French divisions to have landed, with Toulon captured between D+15 and D+20. The other three French divisions were scheduled to land over the course of the following 20 days during which point Marseilles would also be captured. By D+60 all combat and supporting troops were to have been landed.

With the assault forces considered to be sufficiently battle-trained, the decision was taken that they would be assembled near their area of operations in and around Naples, as they could not be withdrawn to North African ports in sufficient time for additional preparations. As such, a fair degree of risk was adopted. The American infantry corps was given only three weeks of ship-to-shore and shore-to-shore training, along with one formal rehearsal. By comparison the forces involved in Neptune spent several months preparing for the operation and had multiple rehearsals to practice what they had learnt. This was certainly not the case for Dragoon, indeed the first of the lead divisions only became available for training on 24 June and the last, the 36th Division, on 8 July, less than seven weeks before the invasion was due to begin. Perhaps most striking of all, the 119 British landing craft which were to be used in the operation only arrived once the final rehearsals had been completed.[28]

25 TNA: WO204/1475, 'Anvil Presentation – 27 December 1943'.

26 'En Provence, L'Armée de Lattre', *Paris Match: L'Histoire*, April 2014, pp.54-59; 'Opération DRAGOON: Le Débarquement de Provence', *Deuxième Guerre Mondiale* (Numero 23; Decembre-Janvier 2009), pp.48-55.

27 De Lattre de Tassigny, Jean, *History of the French First Army* (London: George Allen and Unwin, 1952), pp.30-31.

28 TNA: ADM199/865,Vice Admiral H.K. Hewitt, US Navy, 'Invasion of Southern France: Report of the Naval Commander, Western Task Force', November 1944, pp.166-167.

One element of the plan which did receive much greater attention involved the tackling of key German defences. It was recognised that prior to the landings it would be necessary to neutralise the sites on the Ile d'Hyères and at a few other points. Two missions were proposed involving French commandos, Operation Romeo directed at Cap Nègre on the western flank of the main invasion, where a large group landed to destroy German artillery emplacements, and Operation Rosie which involved an attack at Pointe de l'Esquillon. In a further operation, named Sitka, which was to involve the US-Canadian 1st Special Service Force, the offshore islands of Port Cros and Levant off Ile d'Hyères were to be captured in order to protect the beachhead. As had been the case at Pointe du Hoc during the invasion of Normandy, this special force trained to scale the steep 40-50 feet cliffs of the beachless islands; unlike the Rangers further north, they landed unopposed at around midnight on D-Day and were able to secure their objectives by the day's end.[29]

With General Eisenhower having agreeing to release aircraft and gliders, the maritime invasion force was to be supported by Operation Dove, an airborne assault in the Le Muy area by the 1st Airborne Task Force commanded by General Robert T. Fredericks. Referred to as 'Rugby Force' this consisted of the British 2nd Independent Parachute Brigade, the US 517th Parachute Regimental Combat Team, and a composite US parachute/glider regimental combat team formed from the 509th Parachute Infantry Battalion, the glider-deployed 550th Airborne Infantry Battalion, and the 1st Battalion, 551st Parachute Infantry Regiment. It was very much a provisional airborne division, which was formed and assembled in the Rome area; with there being very little prior knowledge of one another, its troops continued training until just before the final loading for departure.

Supporting all of this was a major deception plan, Operation Span, carried out by the Office of Strategic Services (OSS), which was intended to shield the main invasion. This included a series of dummy parachute drops further to the east of the projected landing zones supported by a mock invasion fleet moving past Genoa to Cannes, led by the US Navy Reserve officer and film star Douglas Fairbanks Jr. Opinion differs as to the effect of this plan; 'Axis Sally', one of the propaganda stations broadcasting into Allied-held Italy, reported that a warm welcome was waiting for the invasion force in Genoa and it seems reasonable to conclude that the deception plan did have some impact even if the defenders were not completely surprised by what followed. Supporting the activities of OSS, the initial December 1943 briefing made specific reference to the role within the operation of the Resistance although it also stressed that "assistance rendered by these groups are considered as a bonus, however, and no part of the plan is dependent upon them for success".[30]

Inevitably for an amphibious invasion, the maritime component was central to the plan. The supporting naval force was organised into four attack groups, each commanded by an American rear-admiral, three for the assault divisions plus one carrying the commandos who were to carry out the special flank operations. It comprised 881 warships, cargo vessels and major landing craft of which 65 percent came from the United States Navy, one-third from the Royal Navy and the remainder from other Allied nations. In addition there were 1,370 smaller vessels employed in the operation; this included 80

29 National Archives and Records Administration, Maryland, United States (hereafter 'NARA'): (RG319, Box 156), 'Invasion of Southern France, Aug 15-28, 1944', Office of the Chief of Military History, n.d., pp.38-41.

30 TNA: WO204/1475, 'Anvil Presentation – 27 December 1943'.

of the highly sought-after LSTs, 120 Landing Craft Tank (LCT) and 120 Landing Craft Infantry (LCI).[31] Each attack group was accompanied by a gun support force drawn from a combination of British, American or French battleships, cruisers and destroyers, a total of 60 warships, which included the French battleship *Lorraine*, British battleship HMS *Ramillies*, and the American battleships USS *Texas*, *Nevada* and *Arkansas*. As naval gunfire support would also be needed for the Seventh Army's anticipated drive on Toulon and Marseilles, it was calculated that one hour would be the maximum time they could fire to assist the initial landings. A British flag officer, Rear-Admiral T.H. Troubridge, had command of the 'Aircraft Carrier Force', referred to as 'Task Force 88', which was made up of seven British and two American escort carriers. Between them they carried 220 fighters which were organised to provide observation for the bombarding warships and close air support for the troops on the beaches.

For the initial assault the 1,300 aircraft – fighter-bombers, medium bombers and heavy bombers – from the XII Tactical Air Command were scheduled to attack prior to the invading forces reaching the shore. This dedicated air support came from Corsica and Sardinia with 35 squadrons of fighters and fighter bombers, 28 squadrons of medium bombers, and from Italy, 30 squadrons of transport and reconnaissance aircraft. In addition there were 84 squadrons of heavy day bombers and a further 10 squadrons of night bombers, all providing cover from their bases in Italy. The planners had called for the early capture of an airfield – of which there were four at Rade d'Hyères, Saint-Raphaël, Cannes and Sète – or the laying of fighter strips which would allow the air component to move from its rear bases. The air capability from the escort carriers provided considerable contingency until such time as this could happen.

The Defenders and their Defences

The task of defending the target sector fell to the Nineteenth Army led by General Friedrich Wiese, an experienced commander and an ardent Nazi, under the general direction of Army Group G.[32] At the time of the initial landings in Normandy there were a total of 12 German divisions in Southern France and one along the Italian border, with various other smaller units dotted around the invasion area. Much as Rommel had proposed to do on the Normandy beaches, the German defenders were told by Wiese that: "… the main line of battle is and remains the beach. Every commander … is ordered to hold his position to the last man and the last bullet".[33] Included within this force there were four mobile divisions, three Panzer and one Panzer Grenadier, which led one senior American commander who had been involved in the operation to argue subsequently that there were adequate numbers to mount a much stronger defence. In Brigadier General Reuben Jenkins' view, "had [they] sealed off 'Dragoon' they could, and undoubtedly would, have maintained themselves in southern and south-western France on the flank of 'Overlord' for a considerable length of time".[34] The degree to which this assessment was commonplace is unclear but, combined with

31 Roskill, *The War at Sea: Vol.III, Part II*, pp.87, 89, 90.

32 Mitcham Jr., Samuel W., *Retreat from the Reich: The German Defeat in France, 1944* (Mechanicsburg, PA: Stackpole Books, 2007), pp.161-163.

33 Cited in Boog, Horst, Krebs, Gerhard, and Vogel, Detlef, *Germany and the Second World War: Volume VII, The Strategic Air War in Europe and the War in the West and East Asia 1943-1944/5* (Oxford: Clarendon Press, 2006), p.647.

34 Jenkins, 'Operation "Dragoon" – Planning and Landing Phase', p.7.

the level of risk that had been adopted both by the planners and during the training, it highlights the potential dangers that were involved.

Such claims also failed to recognise the wider impact of Overlord and the draining effect it had on the German defenders in the south. In reality although there were nearly nine divisions still available as Dragoon was launched, "most of them were depleted, worn out formations which had been transferred to southern France to replace the fresh divisions that were being moved north".[35] Certainly by mid-August all of Wiese's armour had been sent to join the Normandy battle, leaving only the 11th Panzer Division available for an immediate counter-attack. Although it was a formidable force and commanded by the able Major General Wend von Wietersheim, centred around Toulouse it was more than 200 miles from the actual invasion area. There were other military and paramilitary forces but they were of limited value – naval and air coast defence units, logistical, administrative and police formations and numerous 'Ost' battalions filled with East European conscripts and Russians who had agreed to fight against Stalin but were less committed to the idea of fighting in France. This meant that whilst there were theoretically 210,000 troops, their fighting quality was likely to be far less than was the case further to the north. Added to this once Dragoon begain there were only 175 aircraft, 75 tanks and the same number of ships and other vessels facing the huge Allied armada.

There appeared to be some potential advantage to be gained from the defences that had been prepared. Although the priority had been the 'Atlantic Wall', the Germans expected the Allies would invade France in more than one place and had identified the Mediterranean as a possible choice for a landing. As a result 942 permanent positions were built along the southern coasts, supported by approximately 600 artillery pieces. Along the coast from Marseilles to Nice there were in fact a total of 199 batteries and 647 guns, many of which were the 75mm or 88mm varieties; of these only 29 batteries, containing a total of 88 guns, covered the approaches to the landing beaches. A single battery, the heavily fortified position on the St Mandrier Peninsula at Toulon, had 24 of these batteries and a total of 70 guns of various calibres, leaving the remainder of the invasion zone nowhere near as strongly defended.[36] In addition to the fixed defences there were 62,486 land and sea-mines and rows of beach obstacles, but installation of these had only started during the last week of May and in some locations, such as throughout the Delta sector, none were found during the assault.[37] According to the commander of Army Group G, General Johannes Blaskowitz, "The fortifying of the South Coast was severely restricted in favour of" the Channel and Atlantic fronts. No heavy installations were erected except for the existing French works. Typical defences were water obstacles, concrete walls on the beaches, and mining of the deeper water. The defenses (sic) themselves were only field fortifications or a little better".[38] With inadequate defences and insufficient troops, there was plenty of reason to doubt the ability of the German commanders to conduct an effective response.

Despite the efforts of OSS, an advantage the German defenders did hold was their success in anticipating when and where the invasion would take place. At this stage there were still around 200 German aircraft in the sector, and Luftwaffe aerial reconnaissance of Allied

35 Wilt, Alan, 'The Summer of 1944: A Comparison of Overlord and Anvil/Dragoon', *Journal of Strategic Studies* (Vol.4 No.2; 1981), pp.190-191.

36 TNA: ADM199/865, Hewitt, 'Invasion of Southern France…', p.139.

37 Ibid., p.144.

38 Blaskowitz, Generaloberst Johannes, 'German Reaction to the Invasion of Southern France', *Foreign Military Studies* (A-868; 1945), p.2.

shipping together with the knowledge of the withdrawal of the VI Corps from the Italian theatre led Wiese to expect an amphibious assault in the area east of Marseilles and Toulon. By 7 August, Army Group G headquarters had reported that heavy air attacks indicated a landing would take place somewhere along the 150 mile coastline between the Rhône and Var rivers. There were also numerous rumours from sources within the Resistance and amongst the local population pointing to 15 August, Napoleon's birthday, as the invasion date. This supported reports being received from Axis agents who could see the convoys forming up in Italian and Corsican waters and warned that an attack was coming.

The evidence clearly shows that Dragoon came as no real surprise. The problem for the Germans was a lack of available manpower and firepower to respond, and the defenders were in no real position to halt or even slow down the Allies.[39] The progress of the armoured reserves was much restricted, in large part by the ability of 'Ultra' signals intelligence to reveal the German planning, but also as a result of a combination of fuel and transport shortages and the activities of the Resistance. The really critical factor, however, was a massive Allied air campaign which, starting on 5 August, began to target the German defences with a thorough plan for demolishing all roads, railroads, bridges, airfields and beach defences running from 100 miles west of Marseilles to the east of Genoa. As part of the Operation Span deception, and to encourage the Germans to arrive at an inaccurate assessment, particular attention was given to the Italian targets – so much so that at first light on 15 August, German defenders in the area were put on full alert and waiting for an attack. They did not know at this stage that the real focus was elsewhere and over the rivers Rhône, Durance and Var, only one crossing point survived.[40] This meant that what few reinforcements the Germans had kept in Southern France never arrived and the battle that followed was a hugely uneven one.

The Assault

H-Hour for Operation Dragoon had been set at 0800 on 15 August 1944, a compromise between two key strategic requirements. The first pointed to the landings taking place sufficiently late to allow aerial and naval bombardment to destroy or render inoperable the German defences. At the same time, however, sufficient daylight was needed to ensure unloading and allow for the establishment of a firm beachhead with adequate defenders to repel any potential counter-attack. Added to this were considerations relating to the shallow depth of coastal defences and the need to minimise the alert period available to the defenders. Also factored into the decision was the probable absence of enemy naval forces and insights that had been gained during Neptune.

With Wilson in overall charge, and the French II Corps notwithstanding, all of the senior commanders were American: Major General 'Sandy' Patch was responsible for all land forces and the 11 divisions of the Seventh Army and was responsible for all land forces; Vice-Admiral Henry Hewitt, who was amongst the most experienced senior naval officers, led the amphibious operations; Major General Gordon Saville had command of the Tactical Air Forces; and Major General Nathan Twining was in charge of the Strategic Air Forces. The US 6th Army Group, also known as the Southern Group of Armies and as 'Dragoon Force', was created in Corsica and activated on 1 August 1944 to consolidate the combined French and American forces. This was commanded by Lieutenant General

39 Wilt, 'The Summer of 1944...', p.192.

40 Roskill, *The War at Sea: Vol.III, Part II*, p.93.

Jacob L. Devers, who was in addition the deputy Mediterranean theatre commander. On 19 September he would take command of the Seventh Army and the re-designated First French Army when the transfer of this operation from the Mediterranean to the European theatre was completed.

With the limited dock space that was available in Italy and North Africa, the loading of the convoys of Liberty transport ships had been planned so that approximately 150 would be ready by 10 August. It was this advanced preparation which had, in large part, helped halt the very final attempts by the British leadership to move the invasion elsewhere. It also provided the German commanders, through their dockside agents, with plenty of advance notice that the Allies were coming. The clear benefit of this decision was, however, that it also meant the convoys were all loaded on time and able to arrive on schedule. Assisted by a slight haze which formed on the evening of 14 August, effectively hiding them from German reconnaissance aircraft, they assembled at a distance from the French coast. Very early the following morning, and sailing at maximum speed, the invasion force moved towards the beachheads. Few mines and little opposition were encountered; the minesweeper HMS *Antares* was amongst those which emerged unscathed aside from "sporadic shelling from coastal batteries".[41] The small number of German vessels in and around the assault area on D-Day, fewer than 10 small escort or patrol craft, were all quickly destroyed – a pattern that was repeated through the days that followed.[42] The three German U-boats that remained at Toulon fared little better; indeed only one had been able to put to sea by 17 August and four days later it ran aground without having achieved any successes against the huge Allied naval task force.[43] Before the landing craft began moving troops to the shore, the naval gunfire support from Allied ships commenced. As one account put it, "the notable disinterest of the German Air Force was advantageous in allowing the force cover to be reduced to one section of aircraft".[44]

For the invading troops, the experience of those landing in the Camel sector was typical of the operation.[45] Drawn from the 36th US Infantry Division, this had as its target beaches in the Saint-Raphaël to Anthéor area, the two for the initial assault being designated as Blue and Green. The first was a sandy beach only 80 yards in length and unsuitable for vehicles but believed to have no mines or obstructions and to be defended by only a small number of machine gun positions and pillboxes. The second beach, Green, was longer at 840 yards but only one quarter was accessible and vehicles would require matting to be placed to allow them to get off the landing area and move inland through the single available exit. The Germans had a series of pillboxes containing anti-tank machine guns guarding this beach along with a battery of five 150mm guns. With both these first two beaches in effect being suitable for landing only personnel and limited amounts of equipment, a third was required. Red, which was close to the small port of Saint-Raphaël, was more than three times the length of Green. It was also, however, much more heavily defended with an anti-tank wall and ditch blocking all exits, and barbed wire and mines along with supporting concrete obstacles obstructing all the seaward approaches. A final beach, Yellow, was also identified although this was considered to be too heavily defended

41 NARA: Commanding Officer HMS *Antares* (Lieutenant-Commander A.H. Dirck), 'Operation Dragoon', 29 August 1944, p.2.
42 Roskill, *The War at Sea: Vol.III, Part II*, pp.96-97.
43 Ibid., p.101.
44 NARA: 'Report of Proceedings – Operation Dragoon', 11 September 1944.
45 TNA: ADM199/865, Hewitt, 'Invasion of Southern France…', pp.190-193.

for the assault troops and was to be captured from the landward side. The assault plan called for Blue and Green to be attacked at H-Hour with one battalion assigned to the first and two more to the second; Red was to be tackled six or seven hours later. Three hours after the assault had started it was supposed to have been completed.

Prior to the landing craft transporting the men of the 36th Division ashore, the bombardment phase proved a great success and all targets bar one coastal battery to the east of Saint-Raphaël were destroyed or neutralised by H-Hour.[46] This was despite there being only limited visibility resulting from the morning haze and clouds of dust caused by the explosions. The touchdown of the first wave of troops was also preceded by additional bombardment from rocket boats; these had been used to great effect during the Neptune landings and opened fire eight minutes before the landing, drenching the beaches for four minutes. On the run in and for all of the landings in this sector, no underwater obstacles, mines or barbed wire were encountered and enemy gunfire was sporadic and inaccurate, to the extent that only 13 fire support missions were requested during the day. Nonetheless the decision was taken not to land on Red as had been scheduled, in part as a result of the perceived strength of enemy defences and a failure to breach the underwater obstacles, but also because of the success being encountered elsewhere. By 2015, a little more than 12 hours after the invasion had begun, Yellow was open to limited traffic and the troops ashore prepared to assault the final beach. Red was quickly captured later that evening but delays with the clearance of numerous landmines and opening of the exits areas, plus difficulties encountered by minesweepers operating offshore, meant that it was not opened for Allied traffic until two days later. It took another four days before the planned schedule of unloading was attained.

The landings in the Delta sector should also be mentioned as these emphasised the overwhelming nature of the Allied success. Two task groups were assigned to the Delta Attack Force operation, each carrying an assault force; with Task Group 85.4 arriving 10 miles off its beaches at 0430, it was joined 30 minutes later by Task Group 85.5.[47] The landings were scheduled for H-Hour and the troops coming ashore at Red beach found that the pre-assault bombardment had so completely destroyed German strong points on its flanks and on Pointe de Sardinaux that they were able to make a virtually unopposed landing. Just a single American infantryman was killed, by shellfire, and he proved to be the only casualty from either the Army or Navy. When it was clear that there was no meaningful opposition, the commander ordered that every effort be made to speed up the process of landing troops and vehicles and each wave landed progressively earlier than scheduled. With LSTs coming in close to the beaches, by 1600 all the assault force had landed and was moving inland. With so little opposition being encountered on the beaches, the attack in this sector was over almost as soon as it had begun.

Elsewhere Rugby Force faced more of a challenge, not so much as a result of the quality or quantity of the German defenders but rather due to the local weather conditions which resulted in much reduced visibility. Seriously hampered by fog which obscured the landing and drop zones, as had been the case during Neptune not all of the scheduled drops went as expected. Even so, some of the mistakes had unexpected benefits as one of the official histories noted:

46 Ibid.

47 NARA: Commander Task Group 85.4, 'Report of Assault against Southern France of 15 August 1944', 8 September 1944; ibid., Commander Task Group 85.5, 'Action Report of Delta Attack Force, Green Beach Assault Group, 14 September 1944.

> About 0430 on D-Day one serial of 29 planes became confused by ground fog and dropped its load at the wrong point. Thus two full batteries and parts of two others of the 463rd Parachute Field Artillery Battalion landed about three miles south of St Tropez near enemy coastal installations and in the largest area of Allied bombers and naval guns. These paratroopers were considerably shaken up by the bombardment of their own forces but suffered no casualties. They managed to assemble, put five guns in operation, and capture one enemy anti-aircraft battery, two coastal batteries, and a garrison of 240 Germans. Some of the paratroopers moved on, entered St Tropez, and occupied the town. When forward troops of the 15th Regiment reached St Tropez they found the paratroopers attacking the last German defenders in the town strong point, known as the Citadel. The 1st Airborne Task Force had accomplished its mission and a little more.[48]

Within 18 hours 9,099 troops, 213 artillery pieces and anti-tank guns and 221 vehicles had been flown over 200 miles across the Mediterranean and landed by parachute and glider in enemy-held territory. All of the assigned missions had been accomplished within 48 hours. Airborne task force losses included 560 killed, wounded and missing, and 283 jump and glider casualties. The role they played would be described post-war as one of the most successful of its kind.

For the German defenders the target areas had been covered by only one grenadier regiment from the 242nd Infantry Division and another from the 148th Infantry Division, both under the command of Lieutenant General Ferdinand Neuling's LXII Corps. Located at Draguignan to the north of the invasion beaches, he was captured by the airborne troops along with most of his corps staff shortly after the initial assault had begun. Wiese sent a provisional force to the invasion zone under Major General Richard von Schwerin and including elements of three infantry divisions, using an inland route. It never developed any cohesion or fighting force, nor were the German troops able to concentrate their defences as they clashed with the airborne forces and elements of 36th and 45th Divisions moving rapidly inland. Over 94,000 troops and 11,000 vehicles were landed on the first day; by its conclusion, reports indicated a total of 95 American fatalities and 385 wounded, with 2,300 German prisoners. Despite the British misgivings about the operation and its contribution to the Allied 'grand strategy' for defeating German, the invasion of Southern France had resulted in an overwhelmingly positive outcome.

Conclusion

Having completed the landings with little resistance or incident, Truscott sought to exploit his potentially overwhelming advantage. On 17 August German High Command ordered a general withdrawal from Southern France with the Nineteenth Army being ordered to head north up the Rhône Valley. With parts of three divisions providing a screening force, the Germans began a full-scale retreat. Only the substantial garrisons at Marseilles and Toulon, of 13,000 and 18,000 men respectively, were told to remain and fight to the last. As a result of the Allies' superiority in signals intelligence, Patch read the two key withdrawal messages at about the same time as Wiese.[49] In response he

48 'Invasion of Southern France, Aug 15-28, 1944', pp.43-46.

49 Boog et al, *Germany and the Second World War: Volume VII*, pp.656-657.

established a small mobile force consisting of a motorized infantry battalion, a cavalry reconnaissance squadron, field artillery, three tank or tank destroyer companies and an engineer company. Under the command of Brigadier General Frederick B. Butler, and referred to as the 'Butler Task Force', this was ordered to drive the advance forward, swing west and seize key terrain – high ground northeast of Montelimar – which would block the only effective escape route up the Rhône Valley.[50]

As Devers later wrote, "this was obviously a vital decision, a tremendous risk in view of the great number of German troops this small force might have to engage, but to Truscott it was worth the gamble. His judgement was to be sustained by astounding results".[51] The battle for Montelimar, an unanticipated but now key strategic point, lasted for several days and the attacking American forces suffered their largest casualties with 1,575 men – mostly from the 36th Division – killed, wounded or missing.[52] For these losses, the opposing Nineteenth Army had been largely destroyed as a fighting force with its vehicles, troops and horses littering 20 miles of approach roads; during the first five days of Dragoon half of the available defending forces in Army Group G had been encircled, captured or killed and this figure would rise to more than 150,000 by the end of the campaign. Allied forces pushed on at a rapid pace as in little more than a month, 380,000 troops were landed. Within a week of the initial assault the city of Grenoble had been liberated, at a distance of over 190 miles from the beaches. On 12 September, patrols from Seventh Army made contact with General Patton's Third Army at Châtillon-sur-Seine near Dijon having travelled 400 miles from their original landing point.

Despite the overwhelming nature of the German losses, the outcome of the campaign has remained unclear with questions about who could claim the victory.[53] Politically the operation had proven a great success. The French formed a full army to fight through France and, in so doing, the 'stain' of their 1940 defeat was in large part removed. This strengthening of the Allied alliance came, however, at the cost of strained relations with the British. In his diary, Brooke gave the landings only the briefest of mentions noting merely that it seemed "to be going well".[54] Churchill was never reconciled to the assault on the Southern French shores despite the fact that the rapidity of the successes pleasantly surprised him. Indeed the pace of the advance if anything justified his dislike of what he viewed to be a "futile joyride" which failed to divert German troops away from the Overlord battles. He believed that the capture of Rome and the breaking of German defensive positions in Italy had achieved much of what it had been hoped that Anvil would precipitate, restoring the momentum of another front and stretching the German ability to respond to the expanding Allied threat. On 20 August he was told that the Americans thought that Dragoon had priority over the Italian campaign, confirmation of something that the previous months had always seemed to suggest was the case and sealing "the fate of his ambitious Italian project". General Alexander was also convinced that were it not for the removal of the seven divisions, he would have had "more than a sporting chance of destroying the German forces in Italy by the end of 1944 and of being

50 Devers, General Jacob L., 'Operation Dragoon: The Invasion of Southern France', *Military Affairs* (Vol.10, No.2; Summer 1946), pp.34-41.

51 Ibid., p.35.

52 Yeide, Harry and Stout, Mark, *First to the Rhine: The 6th Army Group in World War II* (St Paul, MN: Zenith Press, 2007), pp.83-97.

53 Clarke, Jeffrey J. and Smith, Robert Ross, *The European Theater of Operations: Riviera to the Rhine* (Washington DC: Center of Military History, United States Army, 1993), pp.167-170.

54 Diary Entry, 16 August 1944 in Danchev and Todman (eds.), *War Diaries 1939-1945 – Field Marshal Lord Alanbrooke*, p.581.

in Vienna before the Russians". The seven divisions that were pulled out of the line were only partially compensated by the arrival of the Brazilian 1st Infantry Division, the land forces element of the Brazilian Expeditionary Force.

Militarily, as early as 17 June Field Marshal Gerd von Rundstedt, still then the German Commander-in-Chief in the West, had recommended the evacuation of Southern France; after the success of Neptune it made sense for German forces to withdraw to prepare for the defence of Germany proper. Indeed the argument has been made that Dragoon actually helped the German position as it compelled Hitler to agree to the argument that forces should be manoeuvred into better positions, thus ensuring they were prepared to conduct a more effective defence. Several formations did, however, manage to escape into the Vosges and Germany, 'saved' by the long supply lines needed to sustain the attacking Allied forces and an acute shortage of trucks, which restricted tactical movements.[55] The Allied planners had envisaged greater resistance near the landing areas and underestimated transport and fuel needs, which outstripped supply. During the movement phase the American force needed 100,000 gallons of fuel per day; the three beach dumps that had been established following the landing only held 11,000 gallons and there were similar problems with munitions. The majority had to be used to fuel the push on the ports, which was the main reason why the major fighting around Montelimar was the only other significant action between the two sides. In many respects these shortages proved a greater impediment to the advance than did German resistance.

Perhaps the most often cited rationale for the invasion related to the ports. The French had been given the honour of capturing these and General de Lattre's forces compelled the garrisons to surrender, Toulon on 26 August and Marseilles the following day, with both ports captured nearly intact. General Devers, who as Deputy Supreme Allied Commander Mediterranean Theater of Operations had been one of the main supporters of Anvil, later wrote that, "...the capture of these two ports by the French in such a short period of time will go down in history as one of the greatest jobs they accomplished in the war".[56] Completed by D+14, two weeks after the landing rather than D+35 or D+40 as had been anticipated, the harbours were therefore available much sooner than expected. From late August through December 1944 Marseilles received more Allied supplies than any other port; even after Antwerp became operational in January 1945, it still remained the second most important port with 25 percent of the total supplies for the Allied effort being disembarked through Southern France. By the end of the war almost a million troops had disembarked there, the equivalent of 45 divisions, while over four million tons of cargo had been unloaded as monthly supplies provided 30 to 40 percent of Eisenhower's total needs.[57] The American Supreme Commander stated emphatically that the opening of another supply route to help sustain the campaign in North-West Europe, notably during the Battle of the Bulge which began in December 1944, was one of the most significant benefits of the success achieved by Dragoon. Yet there is a powerful counter argument to suggest that his overwhelming belief in the value of Marseilles meant that he did not allocate enough resources to the task of opening up Antwerp earlier.

55 Jenkins, 'Operation "Dragoon" – Planning and Landing Phase', p.9.
56 Devers, 'Operation Dragoon: The Invasion of Southern France', p.34.
57 Wilt, Alan, *War from the Top: German and British Military Decision Making During World War II* (Indianapolis: Indiana University Press, 1990), p.168.

As one of those closely involved in the planning process put it, the invasion of Southern France was not well known because it competed for attention with the offensive in Normandy, resulting in it being labelled a 'secondary attack'.[58] Nonetheless he concluded that it was without parallel in terms of its achievements, an operation which "in daring and speed of manoeuvre [was] unsurpassed". Another account highlighted "the extreme aggressiveness of the principal Allied commanders – always keeping the initiative and constantly adjusting their plans to meet the changing tactical and operational situation".[59] Such claims are accurate in terms of the apparent effect achieved but the more general argument that Dragoon was critical to the war's outcome would appear open to further debate.[60] General Eisenhower wrote post-war that, "There was no development of that period which added more decisively to our advantages or aided us more in accomplishing the final and complete defeat of the German forces than did this secondary attack coming up the Rhône valley".[61] This was perhaps intended as much as a justification of his wartime patronage of the plan as being any genuine military assessment. Indeed the British official historian, in writing about what was almost the final element of the Mediterranean campaign, was almost certainly more balanced in concluding that it had been a tactical success but "the German defence of France south of the Loire was little more than a balloon which, if pricked was bound to collapse".[62] The question that will likely always remain unanswered is what might have happened in Italy if there had been no invasion of Southern France and how, as a result, the war in Europe might have concluded.[63]

Further Reading

The Admiralty's Battle Summary provides a useful starting point for understanding the events of Operation Dragoon. It includes helpful maps, diagrams and organisational charts whilst its appendices, reproduced in full in this volume, include a considerable amount of supporting detail.[64] Another valuable contemporary account is that provided by General Devers which took the form of an address he gave to the American Military Institute in Washington DC in May 1946 and was later published in the highly respected journal *Military Affairs*. In this the senior commander who was centrally involved both with the planning and execution of the operation concluded that, "No operation in our history had up to then produced more decisive, dramatic, swift and far-reaching results at so little cost".[65] His account, which shares much of Eisenhower's positive polemic, does provide a clear eye-witness narrative about the military aspects of the invasion and the campaign that followed. Its only significant omission is a result of when it was written, with there being no reference to the role played by Ultra and Allied intelligence. Added to this there is the American official history, Forrest Pogue's *The Supreme Command*,

58 Jenkins, 'Operation "Dragoon" – Planning and Landing Phase', p.3.
59 Clarke, 'The Champagne Campaign', p.45.
60 Clarke and Smith, *Riviera to the Rhine*, p.194.
61 Eisenhower, Dwight D., *Crusade in Europe* (London: William Heinemann Ltd., 1950), p.322.
62 Jackson et al., *The Mediterranean and Middle East: Volume VI*, p.200.
63 Tucker-Jones, Anthony, *Operation Dragoon: The Liberation of Southern France 1944* (Barnsley: Pen and Sword, 2009), pp.171-181.
64 Admiralty Historical Section, *Battle Summary No.43: Invasion of the South of France: Operation "Dragoon", 15th August 1944* (London: Historical Section, Admiralty, 1950).
65 Devers, 'Operation Dragoon: The Invasion of Southern France', p.41.

which devotes a chapter to the landings and can be easily downloaded from a number of websites.[66] The later account by Jeffrey J. Clarke and Robert Ross Smith, *The European Theater of Operations: Riviera to the Rhine*, offers perhaps the definitive factual account both of the invasion and the subsequent campaign. Written some years after the events to which it refers, it offers an exhaustive and well balanced study. There are also two published British official histories which offer typically well-written accounts as part of far broader studies.[67] The excellent, but difficult to find, translation of the German 'official' history should also be consulted if possible as it provides a detailed 27-page account drawing on a huge range of German and French sources. In so doing it reaches a broadly similar conclusion; the Allies had not destroyed their opponent but "they had won a respectable victory".[68]

The more popular literature covering this aspect of the liberation of Europe is limited.[69] A surprisingly good account comes with William B. Breuer's *Operation Dragoon* which was first published in 1987 and offers a well-researched account including interviews with more than 50 veterans who fought in the battle.[70] The author of 41 nonfiction books published in the United States, Breuer's style was very much populist and, whilst describing himself as a military historian, his writing covered a huge range of subjects including wartime secret missions, the moon landing, sports, political conspiracies and hoaxes, the CIA and FBI, and the global war on terrorism. Nonetheless, and despite its journalist prose and non-footnoted familiar style, this offers an easily readable and informative description of the operation, focussing on airborne events but also examining the landings themselves. Fortunately the scant bibliography was corrected by the most recent publication on the subject, dating from 2009, which itself highlights what it terms as "the curious disregard" for this operation that exists amongst military historians.[71] Anthony Tucker-Jones' excellent *Operation Dragoon: The Liberation of Southern France 1944*, which draws heavily on American archival sources, provides what should be considered as the best single-source account for those with a general interest in learning more about the invasion of Southern France.

66 Pogue, Forrest C., *United States Army in World War II - European Theater of Operations: The Supreme Command* (Washington DC: Office of the Chief of Military History, Department of the Army, 1954), pp.218-230.

67 Roskill, *The War at Sea: Vol.III, Part II*, pp.85-106; Jackson et al., *The Mediterranean and Middle East: Volume VI*, pp.173-200.

68 Boog et al, *Germany and the Second World War: Volume VII*, p.662.

69 The US Army Center of Military History based at Fort McNair in Washington DC has produced 40 illustrated brochures detailing the campaigns fought by the US Army during the Second World War. The volume on the campaign in Southern France concludes that the number of relevant scholarly works is extremely limited; *Southern France: The U.S. Army Campaigns of World War II* (Washington DC: Center for Military History, 1994) [CMH Pub 72-31].

70 Breuer, William B., *Operation Dragoon – The Allied Invasion of the South of France* (Navato, California: Presidio Press, 1987).

71 Tucker-Jones, *Operation Dragoon: The Liberation of Southern France 1944*, p.198.

Bibliography

Southern France: The U.S. Army Campaigns of World War II (Washington DC: Center for Military History, 1994) [CMH Pub 72-31]

Benbow, Tim, *Operation Neptune: The D-Day Landings, 6 June 1944* (Naval Staff Histories of the Second World War) (Solihull: Helion and Company, 2015)

Blaskowitz, Generaloberst Johannes, 'German Reaction to the Invasion of Southern France', *Foreign Military Studies* (A-868; 1945)

Boog, Horst, Krebs, Gerhard, and Vogel, Detlef (eds.), *Germany and the Second World War: Volume VII, The Strategic Air War in Europe and the War in the West and East Asia 1943-1944/5* (Oxford: Clarendon Press, 2006)

Breuer, William B., *Operation Dragoon – The Allied Invasion of the South of France* (Presidio Press: Navato, California, 1987)

Churchill, Winston, *The Second World War* (London: Penguin Books, 1989)

Clarke, Jeffrey J. and Smith, Robert Ross, *The European Theater of Operations: Riviera to the Rhine* (Washington DC: Center of Military History, United States Army, 1993)

Clarke, Jeffrey J., 'The Champagne Campaign', *Military History Quarterly* (Vol.20 No.2; Winter 2008)

Danchev, Alex and Todman, Daniel (eds.), *War Diaries 1939-1945 – Field Marshal Lord Alanbrooke* (London: Phoenix Press, 2002)

Devers, General Jacob L., 'Operation Dragoon: The Invasion of Southern France', *Military Affairs* (Vol.10 No.2; Summer 1946)

Edmonds, Robin, *The Big Three: Churchill, Roosevelt and Stalin in Peace and War* (London: Penguin Books, 1992)

Eisenhower, Dwight D., *Crusade in Europe* (London: William Heinemann Ltd., 1950)

Harrison, Gordon A., *Cross Channel Attack* (Washington DC: Center of Military History, United States Army, 1989)

Jackson, General Sir William with Gleave, Group Captain T.P., *The Mediterranean and Middle East: Volume VI, Victory in the Mediterranean – Part II, June to October 1944* (London: Her Majesty's Stationery Office, 1987)

Jenkins, Brigadier-General Reuben E., 'Operation "Dragoon" – Planning and Landing Phase', *Military Review* (August 1946)

Lovering, Lieutenant Commander T.T.A., *Amphibious Assault: Manoeuvre from the Sea, Amphibious Operations for the Last Century* (Woodbridge: Seafarer Books, 2007)

Mitcham Jr., Samuel W., *Retreat from the Reich: The German Defeat in France, 1944* (Mechanicsburg, PA: Stackpole Books, 2007)

Molony, C.J.C, *The Mediterranean and Middle East, Volume V: The Campaign in Sicily, 1943 and the Campaign in Italy, 3rd September 1943 to 31st March 1944* (London: Her Majesty's Stationery Office, 1973)

Molony, C.J.C, *The Mediterranean and Middle East, Volume VI, Part I: Victory in the Mediterranean: 1st April to 4th June 1944* (London: Her Majesty's Stationery Office, 1984)

Pogue, Forrest C., *United States Army in World War II - European Theater of Operations: The Supreme Command* (Washington DC: Office of the Chief of Military History, Department of the Army, 1954)

Roskill, Captain S.W., *The War at Sea: Vol.III, The Offensive, Part II, 1st June 1944 – 14th August 1944* (London: Her Majesty's Stationery Office, 1961)

Stewart, Andrew, *Caen Controversy: The Battle for Sword Beach 1944* (Solihull: Helion and Company, 2014)

Stanton, W.I., 'Could WW2 Have Ended in 1944: Was Anvil a Big Mistake?', *Army Quarterly and Defense Journal* (No.122; July 1992)

De Tassigny, Jean de Lattre, *History of the French First Army* (London: George Allen and Unwin, 1952)

Tucker-Jones, Anthony, *Operation Dragoon: The Liberation of Southern France 1944* (Barnsley: Pen and Sword, 2009)

Weiss, Steve, 'The Invasion of Southern France: Operation ANVIL-DRAGOON, August 1944', in Lovering, Lieutenant Commander T.T.A., RN (ed.), *Amphibious Assault: Manoeuvre from the Sea, Amphibious Operations for the Last Century* (Woodbridge: Seafarer Books, 2007)

Wilmot, Chester, *The Struggle for Europe* (London: Collins, 1952)

Wilt, Alan, 'The Summer of 1944: A Comparison of Overlord and Anvil/Dragoon', *Journal of Strategic Studies* (Vol.4 No.2; 1981)

Wilt, Alan, *War from the Top: German and British Military Decision Making During World War II* (Indianapolis: Indiana University Press, 1990)

Yeide, Harry and Stout, Mark, *First to the Rhine: The 6th Army Group in World War II* (St Paul, MN: Zenith Press, 2007)

Sources

M05662/45.	1. C.-in-C. Mediterranean's Despatch.
	2. Report of Vice-Admiral Hewitt, U.S.N.—This is the main source and as it is frequently quoted in the narrative, for the sake of brevity it is referred to as " H."
M057745/45.	Vice-Admiral Hewitt's Operation Plan with Annexes A–S.
M057950/44.	Preliminary report of Rear-Admiral Troubridge (C.T.F.88).
M010202/44.	1. Final report of Rear-Admiral Troubridge.
	2. Rear-Admiral Troubridge's Operation Orders.
	3. Individual Rs. of P. of certain of Admiral Troubridge's ships, i.e., *Emperor, Khedive, Pursuer, Searcher, Attacker, Colombo* and *Troubridge.*
MO11712/44.	C.-in-C. Mediterranean's comments on Rear-Admiral Troubridge's report.
M04533/45.	R. of P. *Hunter.*
M04532/45.	R. of P. *Stalker.*
M011533/44.	R. of P. *Stalker* (continuation) also R. of P. *Dido* and R. of P. *Colombo* (duplicate).
MO107/45.	Report of Rear-Admiral Mansfield (C.S.15, C.T.G.84.7) in *Orion* with comments by Rear-Admiral Lowry, U.S.N. (C.T...F.84).
M011587/44.	R. of P. *Ramillies.* M011228/44. R. of P. *Aurora.*
M010759/44.	R. of P. *Argonaut.* M058498/44. R. of P. *Ajax.*
M013192/44:	R. of P. *Black Prince.*
M013193/44.	R. of P. *Orion.*
M03316/45.	Loss of L.C.T. 307.
M04531/45.	R. of P. S.O. "F" Support Craft Squadron, and of individual craft.
M09992/45.	R. of P. 5th Minesweeping Flotilla.
M06465/45.	R. of P. 19th Minesweeping Flotilla.
M012172/44.	Action Report. S.C.978.
M06466/45.	Action Report Boat Minesweepers.

Abbreviations

A.A.	Anti-Aircraft.
A.P.D.	American destroyer used as a transport.
A.S.R.C.	Air Sea Rescue Craft.
A.T.A.	Ocean Tug Auxiliary (U.S.).
A.T.R.	Ocean Rescue Tug (U.S.).
B.Y.M.S.	British "Y" Class Minesweeper.
C.-in-C.	Commander-in-Chief.
C.C.S.	Combined Chiefs of Staff.
Cort Div.	Escort Division (U.S.).
C.O.S.	Chief(s) of Staff.
C.O.S.S.A.C.	Chief of Staff to Supreme Allied Commander (for Operation "Overlord").
C.S.15	Flag Officer Commanding 15th Cruiser Squadron.
C.T.F.	Commander Task Force.
C.T.G.	Commander Task Group.
D Day	The day fixed for an operation.
D + or –5	Five days after (or before) the date fixed for an operation.
D24	Captain D. 24th Destroyer Flotilla.
DD Tanks	Amphibious Tanks.
Des. Div.	Destroyer Division (U.S.).
D.U.K.W.S.	Amphibious Trucks, commonly called Ducks.
E-Boat	German motor torpedo boat.
F.D.T.	Fighter Defence Tender = L.S.F.
F.F.I.	French Resistance Movement (Maquis).
F.T.	Fleet Tender.
G.C.I.	Ground Control Interception.

H. Hour	The exact hour fixed for the commencement of an operation.
H.Q.	Headquarters.
J.S.M.	Joint Staff Mission (in Washington).
L.C.A.	Landing Craft Assault.
L.C.C.	”–” Control.
L.C.F.	”–” Flak.
L.C.G.	”–” Gun.
L.C.H.	”–” Headquarters.
L.C.I.	”–” Infantry.
L.C.M.	”–” Mechanized.
L.C.M.(R)	”–” ” (Rocket).
L.C.M.(S)	”–” ” (Smoke).
L.C.N.	”–” Navigation.
L.C.P.(R)	”–” Personnel (Ramped).
L.C.R.	”–” Rubber.
L.C.S.	”–” Support.
L.C.T.	”–” Tank.
L.C.T.(R)	”–” ”–” (Rocket).
L.C.V.P.	”–” Vehicle Personnel,
L.S.C.	Landing Ship Carrier.
L.S.D.	”–” Dock.
L.S.E.	”–” Emergency Repair.
L.S.F.	”–” Fighter Direction = F.D.T.
L.S.G.	”–” Gantry.
L.S.I.	”–” Infantry.
L.S.P.	”–” Personnel.
L.S.T.	”–” Tank.
M.A.S.	Italian Motor Torpedo Boat.
M.F.V.	Motor Fishing Vessel.
Min. Div.	Minesweeping Division (U.S.).
Min. Ron.	Minesweeping Squadron (U.S.).
M.L.	Motor Launch.
M/S	Minesweeping.

N.C.W.T.F.	Naval Commander Western Task Force.
P.C.	Patrol Craft (U.S.).
P.T.	American Motor Torpedo Boat.
R.C.T.	Regimental Combat Team (U. S.) = Brigade.
R. of P.	Report of Proceedings.
S.A.C. MED.	Supreme Allied Commander Mediterranean Theatre.
S.C.	Submarine Chaser (U.S.).
S.C.A.E.F.	Supreme Commander Allied Expeditionary Force (Operation "Overlord").
S.H.A.E.F.	Supreme Headquarters Allied Expeditionary Force (Operation "Overlord").
S.I.C.	Secret Intelligence Committee.
S.O.	Senior Officer.
T.F.	Task Force.
T.G.	Task Group.
U. Boat	German Submarine.
U.S.N.	United States Navy.
U.S.S.	United States Ship.
Y.F.	Covered Lighter (U.S.).
Y.M.S.	"Y" Class Minesweeper (U.S.).
Y.T.L.	Small Harbour Tug (U.S.)

Introduction

In August, 1943, the Prime Minister, Mr. Churchill, with the British Chiefs of Staff, met President Roosevelt and the American Chiefs of Staff at Quebec. The future course of the war was considered and it was decided that the invasion of Normandy, Operation "Overlord," should be carried out at the beginning of May, 1944, with an assault strength of three divisions. With the object of drawing off German forces from the north of France, and to contain those already in the south during the critical early days of the" Overlord" build up, it was further decided to carry out an operation in southern France early in May, 1944, to which was later given the code name "Anvil" and General Eisenhower, the Supreme Allied Commander in the Mediterranean, was instructed to submit an appreciation of the outline of plans to the Combined Chiefs of Staff by 1st November, 1943 (*see* C.O.S. (43) 509 (0)).

General Eisenhower made his report in October, 1943, and in it stated that even if "Anvil" was not mounted it would still be possible to tie down the German divisions defending the Riviera coast by the threat of landing. Then if "Overlord" went well it would later be possible to land French forces in the South without the necessity of an assault.

He considered that if "Anvil" was carried out it would be essential to capture a port, preferably Toulon, within range of single engined fighters based on Corsica, so that the limitations of the shipping available would not retard the build-up.

Between 22nd November, 1943, and 6th December, 1943, a series of conferences was held at Cairo and Teheran by President Roosevelt and Mr. Churchill, together with the British and American Chiefs of Staff; Marshal Stalin and his staff attended the meeting at Teheran and particularly pressed for the mounting of the second front in France, of which operation "Anvil" formed part, with all speed.

The British Chiefs of Staff required that if "Anvil" was to be carried out the assault should be made with a minimum of two divisions. As there was not sufficient assault shipping for this in the Mediterranean, ships would have to be sent there at the expense of other operations; but there was to be no subtraction from the "Overlord" forces. The United States Chiefs of Staff agreed and the joint planners were directed to examine the proposals. They reported (*see* C.C.S.424) on 5th December, 1943, that at least two divisions would be required for the assault, and they also gave estimates of the additional ships and craft which the Supreme Commander in the Mediterranean would need. These included 9-12 Escort Carriers, six Anti-Aircraft Cruisers, three Combat Loaders, 26 L.S.T., and 31 L.C.T.

These conclusions were submitted to the President, the Prime Minister, and Marshal Stalin who gave them their approval, and directions were sent to General Eisenhower on 6th December, 1943, to prepare an outline plan (FAN 283 No. T.O.O.) as quickly as possible for a two divisional assault on the south of France to be launched in May, 1944.

It is important to note here that the planning staff at Teheran worked on the assumption that by the time "Anvil" was launched the allied armies in Italy would have reached the Pisa-Rimini line and would be able to exert strong pressure on the enemy.

Shortly after the Teheran meeting there occurred big changes in the allied commands in the Mediterranean. General Eisenhower was appointed Supreme Commander of the Allied Expeditionary Force which was to land in Normandy (S.C.A.E.F.) and was relieved in the Mediterranean by General Sir Henry Maitland Wilson on 24th December, 1943. At the same time General Sir Bernard Montgomery relinquished command of the Eighth Army and became General Eisenhower's Military Commander-in-Chief and also commanded the Twenty-first Army Group. General Sir Harold Alexander was appointed Commander-in-Chief, Italy, under the Supreme Commander, General Wilson. On 28th December, 1943, Admiral Sir John Cunningham, Naval Commander-in-Chief, Mediterranean, nominated Vice-Admiral H. K. Hewitt, U.S.N., as the Naval Commander, Western Task Force (N.C.W.T.F.). Admiral Hewitt was to command the naval side of "Anvil" and was entrusted with the task of drawing up the detailed naval plan.

General Eisenhower, on establishing himself at his headquarters in London, and after reviewing the "Overlord" plan with his Commanders-in-Chief, Admiral Ramsay, General Montgomery and Air Marshal Leigh-Mallory, sent a signal to the British and American Chiefs of Staff that the "Overlord" assault should be increased from three to five divisions (B.33/M.37 232300/Jan.). He was reluctant to see the "Anvil" assault reduced below two divisions, but if it were impossible to provide sufficient resources for this then he would accept a reduction in "Anvil." It should here be emphasised that there was no difficulty in supplying the troops necessary for the two operations. The difficulty lay in transporting them to the point of attack owing to the shortage of assault shipping. General Eisenhower added that he was prepared to postpone the "Overlord" assault until early June if this delay would result in the provision of the additional shipping.

On 26th January, 1944, the British Chiefs of Staff sent a message (C.O.S.(W) 1904 261130/Jan) to the American Chiefs of Staff expressing general agreement with General Eisenhower and stating that they were examining the extent to which the Supreme Commander's requirements could be met from British sources.

Meanwhile, the campaign in Italy had not been going entirely according to plan. German demolitions and the weather had considerably slowed down the advance. The Anzio landing, though successful, was unable to make headway against the German resistance, whilst the maintenance of this force provided an extra commitment for the Mediterranean assault shipping. Uncertainty as to how long this situation would continue rendered difficult any firm plan for "Anvil." Exchanges of views continuously took place on this subject between the British and American Chiefs of Staff, and it was finally decided that planning for "Anvil" should continue but no preparations for it were to be made to the detriment of operations in Italy, which were to have priority (C.O.S.(W) 1168 231740 and J.S.M.1538 252317/Feb.).

On 19th March, 1944, General Wilson submitted his views on the situation. He said that no fresh attack in Italy could be made before April 15th. He was confident that this attack would be successful but did not expect the junction with the army at Anzio before 15th May. If it were decided to mount "Anvil" the earliest date would be late July. As the result of these views further discussion took place between Washington and London as to whether or not "Anvil" should be carried out, and it was not until 2nd July that this was finally decided upon and orders were given to General Wilson to launch the assault on 15th August, 1944, with three divisions (C.O.S. Med. 139 021120/July).

On 27th July, for security reasons, the code name of the operation was changed from "Anvil" to "Dragoon" and detailed planning, which had never entirely ceased, was now redoubled in intensity at the various headquarters in the Mediterranean.

It will be seen from the foregoing that in the months which had elapsed since the inception of "Anvil" at the Quebec meeting in August, 1943, the object of the operation had changed. The original intention of the Allied Chiefs of Staff was that the landing on the Riviera should take place soon after the assault on the Normandy beaches with the object of drawing to the south some of the German divisions opposing General Eisenhower. The tenacious resistance offered by the German army in Italy rendered necessary a postponement of the southern landing, and when it was finally decided to undertake it the defeat of the enemy in Northern France had been accomplished. The successful achievement of "Overlord" had now raised a new American requirement for another large port in France in order to land 35 divisions which were ready in the U.S.A. and which could not be deployed through the northern ports. Operation "Dragoon," if successful, would achieve this.

In the following chapters a detailed account is given of the planning and preparations, the assault and the follow up for operation "Dragoon." The operation took place, as planned, on 15th August, 1944, three American divisions landing on the beaches to the eastward of Toulon preceded by an airborne division and by commando landings. The build-up consisted of seven French divisions two of which were armoured, the whole comprising the Seventh Army under Lieutenant General Patch. While a portion of this army operated against Toulon and Marseilles, both of which ports fell on 28th August, the bulk of the Allied forces advanced up the Rhône valley driving before them the German divisions, which had opposed them. So rapid was the advance, and so little resistance were the Germans able to offer, that Lyons was entered on 3rd September and Dijon on 11th September, while Vesoul was captured on 12th September. On 15th September, one month after the landing, the Seventh Army was in line with General Eisenhower's forces in Northern France and General Wilson, Supreme Allied Commander Mediterranean, then relinquished the direction of General Patch's army in favour of General Eisenhower.

I

PLANNING AND PREPARATIONS

1. Outline Plan of Operation "Dragoon"[1]

The assault was to be carried out by the U.S. 6th Corps, commanded by Major-General Truscott and comprising the 36th, 45th and 3rd Divisions from North to South, landing at Agay, St. Raphael, Sainte Maxime, and in the Bays of Pampelonne and Cavalaire, and by a French armoured brigade, which was to be put ashore near St. Raphael. It was timed for 0800 on 15th August, 1944.

In the early hours of that morning French Commandos were to land on Cape Nègre to capture batteries which could enfilade the Cavalaire beaches, and American commandos, under Colonel Waller, were to land on the islands of Levant and Port Cros to capture batteries, which could command the transport and naval bombardment areas. Another detachment of commandos was to land before daylight to the south of La Napoule Gulf to block the roads leading from Cannes to St. Raphael.

The assault was also to be preceded by the dropping of an airborne division, commanded by Brigadier-General Frederick, which was to emplane at airfields near Rome. Included in this division were the only British troops taking part in the operation, the 2nd Parachute Brigade. The airborne division, which was to land in the vicinity of Le Muy, had the mission of blocking the movement of enemy reserves into the assault area from the north and north-west. The infantry divisions were to move inland as rapidly as possible, making contact with the airborne force, secure the beach head, and extend it to a depth of about 14 miles by D+1.

The follow up was to commence on D+1 and was to be by French army B, under General de Lattre de Tassigny, composed of the 1st Corps under General Martin which consisted of the 2nd and 4th Moroccan Divisions and the 5th Armoured Division, while the 2nd Corps under General de Larminat contained the 1st Motorised Division, the 3rd Algerian Division, the 9th Colonial Division and the 1st Armoured Division. The 2nd Corps less the 9th Division was to be ashore by D+5 and the remaining division was to land by D+9. The French troops were to pass through the left of the Americans and proceed to the capture of Toulon and Marseilles. The 1st Corps was to land from D+20. The whole Seventh Army was under the command of Lieut.-General Patch who had commanded the American forces at Guadalcanal. The detailed naval plan will be considered later.

The Strategical Air Force was under the command of Major-General Twining, and the Tactical Force was commanded by Brigadier-General Saville[2] both of the U.S. Army Air Corps. The Strategical Force, based in Italy, was to carry out a programme of heavy bombing before the assault, aimed at the neutralisation of the enemy's air

1 F.80296, 071900 August and C.O.S. (44) 713 (0) 9th August.

2 C.O.S.(44)713(0). In Admiral Hewitt's operation plan, Annex F. Appendix 1. p. 6, it is stated that the Tactical Air Force was commanded by Major-General Cannon.

power and the disruption of his communications. This bombing had to be carefully integrated with the general air offensive to prevent the enemy from deducing the point selected for the assault. This softening up had begun as early as 29th April with an attack on the harbour at Toulon, and continued with increased intensity from 19th May. Once the assault had been launched the Strategical Air Force would be employed mainly against communications and tactical targets, but airfields would be attacked when necessary. The Tactical Air Force was based in Corsica and Sardinia and had the task of providing close support and cover for the assaulting forces. It was to be augmented by the aircraft from the Carrier Force.

2. Planning

In the Mediterranean naval planning was commenced at the end of December 1943, when Vice-Admiral Hewitt, U.S.N., commanding the 8th U.S. Fleet, was appointed Naval Commander Western Task Force (N.C.W.T.F.) and charged by the C.-in-C. Mediterranean, Admiral Sir John Cunningham, with the task of planning and launching the naval side of operation "Anvil." The experience gained in the invasions of North Africa, Sicily and Italy was of the greatest value. Planning sections of the Army, Navy and Air Force were all established at Bouzareah, just outside Algiers, and when General Patch arrived he established his headquarters in the same place. On 8th July, 1944, Planning H.Q. for the operation followed Allied Force Headquarters to Naples, near where it had been decided to train the three assault divisions. General Patch and Brigadier-General Saville, who had been appointed Air Commander of the expedition, also set up their H.Q. at Naples, as did General Truscott who commanded the 6th Corps and General de Lattre de Tassigny who was in command of the French Army; hence there was no repetition of the difficulties which arose during the planning of the Salerno landing owing to the wide dispersal of the different authorities.

Difficulties, however, there were. In the first place there was no certainty as to the strength of the assault,[1] and it was not until 2nd July that the final order for a three divisional assault was issued. Moreover, until 2nd July the Italian campaign had a priority over preparations for "Anvil" and as most of the available assault craft were engaged in supplying the armies in Italy it was never possible to carry out much training, nor to estimate how many landing craft would be available for the invasion. To carry out a landing with three divisions, additional assault shipping had to be provided from the United States and from General Eisenhower's forces, but the decision to send craft from America was only reached in mid-May, while not until the end of June was the exact number of the craft to be withdrawn from S.H.A.E.F. made known.

Owing to the late decision as to the strength of the assault it is not surprising that the 6th Corps assault plan was not ready before 30th July, and not until then could the final details of the naval plan be worked out and promulgated. As the first of the assault convoys had to sail on 9th August there was not much time. Under these circumstances the naval planning memoranda issued from time to time were of the greatest value in enabling force commanders to draw up their plans before the general plan was finally completed. It was at first intended that the 85th Division at Oran should make a ship to shore assault while the landing of the other two divisions from Naples would be shore

1 See introduction.

to shore.[1] It was eventually decided, however, that the 36th Division should take the place of the 85th so that the whole force would sail from Naples. As a result it was planned that each division would have one Regimental Combat Team (R.C.T.)[2] loaded in combat loaders or L.S.I., one in L.S.T. and the third R.C.T., which would be in reserve, would be embarked in L.C.I. and L.C.T. The naval forces corresponding to the three divisions were named "Alpha," "Delta" and "Camel," while the naval force working with the Commandos was given the name "Sitka." Each of these forces was self-contained and had its own bombardment force, support craft and minesweepers. The aircraft carriers formed a separate force under Rear-Admiral Troubridge, while escorts, anti-U-Boat patrols, screening groups and the Naval Train were under the direct command of Admiral Hewitt, who was to fly his flag in the *Catoctin*.

Early in 1944 Corsica was being developed as an advanced naval supply depot for the invasion, and it was arranged that landing craft convoys should stage in Corsican ports. Airfields in Corsica were also organised so that shore-based single-engine fighters could give cover to the beaches. An amphibious training centre was developed at Salerno where the assault divisions could train with landing craft.

3.

Five different areas in Southern France had been considered as landing places for the invasion—the Cette-Agde area, the Gulf of Fos, the Gulf of Hyères, the Marseilles-Toulon area and the Cavalaire-Agay area. The objections to the Cette-Agde area were that there was no lee for shipping and no port which could shelter deep draught vessels; furthermore the port of Cette was small and could easily have been blocked by the enemy, while the neighbouring beaches were poor, their gradients unsuitable for pontoons, and their exits bad. In addition beach obstacles were more highly developed than in any of the other areas and the country between Cette and Marseilles was difficult and broken by lakes, lagoons, marshes and ditches, which would have hindered the rapid advance of the army. Finally the area was out of range of fighters based on Corsica.

The Gulf of Fos was heavily mined; the beaches were good but the area contained no port capable of maintaining the assault divisions, and the country inland was swampy. The objections to the Gulf of Hyères were the fact that extensive minesweeping would be necessary before the assault, while there would not be sufficient hours of darkness for this to be accomplished; there was lack of sea room for the bombardment forces, and the batteries on the coast and on the islands of Porquerolles, Port Gros and Levant would command the beaches and transport areas. The beaches in the Marseilles-Toulon area were good but it was considered that the strength of the coast defences would make a landing too hazardous.

The Cavalaire-Agay area was eventually chosen as being the most favourable. It was the nearest possible area to Corsica, the sea approach was good and not heavily mined, it was less strongly defended than most landing places on the coast, the beaches were good and three small ports offered shelter and good anchorages for shipping. In addition, the enemy did not appear to expect a landing in this neighbourhood and a bridge-head in this sector would provide a suitable base for the advance on Toulon and Marseilles. On

1 M.05662/45. Admiral Hewitt's report, p. 7.
2 The R.C.T. is the equivalent of a British brigade.

the other hand the country inland was difficult, and an advance of 38 miles would have to be made to reach Toulon. Great stress was laid on the necessity for a rapid advance inland to reach high ground so as to deny to the enemy artillery, positions from which the beaches could be shelled. It was desired that by D+1 the depth of the beachhead should be about fourteen miles and this in fact was attained. The hour for landing the main forces was fixed for 0800. This was a compromise between the need to give adequate time to the bombardment forces for neutralising the defences and the necessity for allowing the maximum of daylight hours for unloading.

Before the landing in Normandy efforts were made to convince the enemy that an assault would be made on Southern France. Later, when it was finally decided to carry out Operation "Dragoon," a strategic deception was adopted to fix the enemy's attention on the Eastern Mediterranean. For this purpose preparations were made for mounting follow-up divisions at ports in the "heel" of Italy, the escort carriers were ordered to the Levant, and the concentration of the bombarding forces at Malta and Taranto and of the assault shipping at Naples was consistent with an intention to carry out an invasion to the east of Italy; to what extent the enemy was deceived is not known.

4. The Gunfire Plan

Admiral Hewitt's criticisms after the Salerno landing of the military insistence on the doctrine of tactical surprise with the corollary that there must be no bombardment of the enemy's positions immediately before a landing, had at length borne fruit. In planning for Operation "Dragoon," it was assumed that the convoys would be sighted and that by midnight on August 14th the enemy would have realised in what region the expedition intended to land. Hence plans were made for a heavy naval bombardment to be carried out from dawn to H-hour.[1] Heavy air attacks were to be made in conjunction with the naval bombardment, and air support would be given during and after the landing. The Air Plan is considered more fully in Section 11.

The bombarding forces consisted of about sixty vessels, battleships, cruisers and destroyers. The weight of the bombardment was, however, limited by the restricted quantity of heavy calibre ammunition available, especially for the French ships, and the necessity of conserving it for the later bombardments of the fortifications of Toulon and Marseilles. The principal targets selected were four heavy coast defence batteries, but light and field batteries were also to receive attention and a comprehensive target list was drawn up so that the Naval Force Commanders could rapidly assign targets to their bombarding ships.

Air spotting had been considerably developed and would be carried out by aircraft from the American cruisers, from the carrier force, and from the Allied Air Forces. Air spotting was to be supplemented by Landing Craft Control (L.C.C.) which, when the target was near the coast, could control the fire from close off shore. The "Sitka" fire support group, after its task of covering the commando landings had been completed, would form a reserve bombardment force which Admiral Hewitt could employ to augment the fire in any desired sector. Owing to the fact that the enemy surface forces were insignificant there was no necessity for providing strong covering forces, and so all the heavy ships available could be used for bombardment.

1 The experience of the Normandy landing had also confirmed the soundness of a preliminary bombardment.

The landing was to be covered by close support fire from destroyers, L.C.G., L.C.T.(R) and from the ship-borne L.C.S., while protection against enemy air attacks on the beaches and shipping would be given by the L.C.F. After the landing the heavy ships would continue to provide supporting fire, and shore fire control parties were to be landed and put into operation as quickly as possible. Elaborate plans were drawn up for the use of smoke as a protection to our ships and forces, and considerable supplies had been built up. Each Force Commander would control the making of smoke in his area, and it was realised that he must decide whether the risk from the enemy was sufficient to justify the loss of visibility and slowing down the work on the beaches which the use of smoke would inevitably entail.

5. Naval Demolition Units

Owing to the fact that off the assault area the hundred fathom line is only from three to six miles from the shore, the area in which the enemy could lay deep minefields was very restricted, but the approaches to the beaches were plentifully strewn with shallow water mines. In addition, access to the beaches was obstructed by concrete pyramids and tetrahedra, usually mined, and in some places by rows of rails or stakes to which explosives were attached. To deal with these obstacles a number of L.C.V.P. had been converted to Apex boats, also known as Drones or Drone boats; these carried 8,000 pounds of high explosive and were remotely controlled. The Apex boats were to precede the assault and were to be guided towards the selected beaches, scuttled and exploded so as to clear a channel through the obstructions. Obstacles which remained after the assault were to be cleared by the use of "Reddy Fox" demolition charges. Another special craft was the "Woofus." This was an L.C.M. converted to fire rockets to clear barbed wire and other obstacles on the beaches. Fifty-four Apex boats and twenty-one Woofus craft were to be used in the assault. Naval Combat demolition units had also been formed to deal with these obstacles. Not much reliance was placed on the Apex boats, and it was assumed that the first boat waves would suffer considerable losses[1] but that the demolition parties, each of which had its own L.C.V.P. would be able to clear channels for the later assault waves as they were to land a few minutes after the assault. These parties also had the duty of assisting the army engineers in their task of clearing the beaches, and in addition they were to operate the Woofus boats.

6. Convoys

The greater part of the assault convoys was to sail from Naples. There were four types of convoy, two fast, one for combat loaders and L.S.I., and one for L.C.I., the medium speed convoys were principally for L.S.T. and the slow for L.C.T. The L.C.I. and L.C.T. convoys were to stage at Ajaccio. The Commandos were in a special L.S.I. convoy (SY1) which was to sail from Naples and stage at Propriano in Corsica. The French armoured brigade was to sail in a special L.S.I. and L.S.T. convoy from Oran. The composition and programmes of the convoys is best shown in tabular form and will be found in *Appendices* C and D,[2] while the convoy routes are shown in Plan 2. The carrier force was to sail from

1 H. p. 302.

2 The numbers of ships shown in convoys in Annex H. to operation plan do not in all respects agree with numbers taking part in the assault shown in H. p. 30. The additional L.S.T., L.C.I., and L.C.T. are accounted for by craft completing repairs quicker

Malta, and the different bombardment forces concentrated at Malta, Taranto, Palermo and Naples. The first follow up convoy of store ships was to sail from Naples and arrive in the assault area during the afternoon of August 15th, closely followed by a convoy of ammunition ships and store ships from Oran. On August 16th two convoys from Taranto were due to arrive containing troops and equipment of the 1st French Infantry Division and 3rd Algerian Infantry Division. Information about the later follow up convoys is not given in the annex to the operation plan.[1]

There had been considerable concern during the planning at the slow speed (5½ knots) of the L.C.T. convoy. This convoy was composed of different types of craft, some of which had been operating for long periods without proper refits. The speed was necessarily that of the slowest craft and was further reduced by the fact that a number of the L.C.T. would be towing smaller craft, such as L.C.M. and L.C.C. Individual approach corridors were arranged for the three main Task Force Commanders, and the assault convoys were to be released to the Force Commanders at points AL AM and AN.[2]

The convoys were to receive the greatest possible protection from the aircraft of the Coastal Air Force and arrangements were made to carry out check sweeps of the Straits of Bonifacio through which most of the convoys had to pass.

7. Logistics

The logistics of the operation reached tremendous proportions. It was necessary hurriedly to establish an amphibious training base at Salerno and to organise ashore at Salerno, Naples, Nisida and Pozzuoli the numerous activities required to support a large number of ships and craft. As Admiral Hewitt remarks "The success of this and other amphibious landings in the Mediterranean has been due in large part to the outstanding support rendered by shore based activities and by repair ships based … at some distance from the area of assault."[3] Advanced naval and air bases were established in Corsica and as no one port in the island was big enough to contain all the necessary services, these had to be divided between a number of different places. Large quantities of fuel of different types had to be provided for the smaller craft and arrangements made for shuttle services to transport this fuel from Corsica and to maintain stocks in the island.

Water had to be supplied in great quantities for the beaches and for ships, as little could be expected ashore in the assault areas. Storage tanks and distilling plants were constructed in Corsica. No less than 26 L.S.T. were equipped as water carriers to supply drinking water over the beaches, but there was a shortage of water carriers, and it was realised that the greatest economy would have to be exercised. It may be noted that the requirements of the army alone during the first five days of the assault amounted to 350,000 gallons. Great quantities of ammunition of different calibres had to be

part in the assault shown in H. p. 30. The additional L.S.T., L.C.I., and L.C.T. are accounted for by craft completing repairs quicker than had been expected, and as stated in H. p. 30 deficiencies were usually due to craft having broken down. Four cruisers and eleven destroyers listed in the operation plan were not in the assault area on D-day; the destroyers were the escorts of D+1 convoys, while the four cruisers remained in reserve at Palermo, and two of them, the Sirius and Omaha, took part in the later stages of the operation. A number of ships belonging to the train remained in ports far from the assault area though their role in the operation was very important.

1 It is stated in Annex H to operation plan p. 2 that detail of follow up convoys is shown in Appendix 5 to this annex, but the copy supplied to the Admiralty contains no Appendix 5.

2 See Plan 2.

3 H. p. 313.

accumulated at suitable ports and plans had to be laid for the carrying out of repairs to ships and craft, particularly to L.C.T. as these craft would have to bear a heavy burden in unloading store ships in the assault area.

Repair ships were based at Naples and Oran and others were stationed at Corsican and Sardinian ports during the early stages of the assault, being due to move to the assault area as soon as this should be considered reasonably safe. In addition three L.S.T. and four L.C.I. had been fitted out as Mother Ships for the smaller craft and these relieved a long felt want. Two 350-ton pontoon dry docks were to accompany the repair ships to the assault area and two British Landing Ships Dock (L.S.D.) were scheduled to take part in the operation. Two British Landing Ships Emergency Repair (L.S.E.) had been requested but only one could be spared, and she did not arrive in the assault area until long after D-day. Organisation had also to be provided for the rapid and orderly unloading of store ships to provide for the increasing degree of maintenance and build up of the forces ashore. This unloading was to be carried out by the L.C.T. and the Army Dukws augmented by 218 L.C.M., of which 170 were loaded on merchant vessels and the remainder on two L.S.G. and one L.S.C.

8. Naval Command and Forces Employed

The naval forces were commanded by Vice-Admiral H. K. Hewitt U.S.N., who was also in command of the army until it was firmly established ashore. Under him were five task force commanders. C.T.F.*84*, "Alpha" Attack Force, was Rear-Admiral Lowry U.S.N., whose gunfire support group was commanded by Rear-Admiral Mansfield flying his flag in the *Orion*. C.T.F.*85*, "Delta" Attack Force, was Rear-Admiral Rodgers, U.S.N., who had under his orders a gunfire support group commanded by Rear-Admiral Bryant, U.S.N., who flew his flag in the *Texas*, and containing a French bombarding force commanded by Rear-Admiral Jaujard in the *Georges Leygues*. C.T.F.*87*, "Camel" Attack Force, was Rear-Admiral Lewis U.S.N.,[1] whose gunfire support commander, Rear-Admiral Deyo, U.S.N., flew his flag in the *Tuscaloosa*. C.T.F.*86*, "Sitka" Assault Force, and subsequently support force commander was Rear-Admiral Davidson, U.S.N. The combat loaders and transports were under the general command of Commodore Edgar, U.S.N. The Carrier Squadron, Task Force 88, was commanded by Rear-Admiral Troubridge,[2] whose second-in-command was Rear-Admiral Durgin, U.S.N., flying his flag in the *Tulagi*. Admiral Hewitt's flagship was the *Catoctin*. The Assault Force Commanders wore their flags in the *Duane* (Alpha) *Biscayne* (Delta) and *Bayfield* (Camel) while Admiral Davidson's flagship was the *Augusta* and that of Admiral Troubridge the *Royalist*.

A number of formations remained under the direct command of Admiral Hewitt. These comprised a division of minesweepers, the special operations group, the screening group consisting of 18 P.T. boats, the anti-submarine and convoy control group, which contained twelve flotillas of destroyers and escort vessels, and finally the Naval Train.[3]

1 Rear-Admiral Moon who had been designated for this command died ten days before the landing and was succeeded by Admiral Lewis, at that time Chief of Staff to Admiral Hewitt. (Information verbally from Admiral Lewis.)

2 Rear-Admiral Bissett, who had been in command of the carriers and who had trained the squadron, was relieved owing to illness shortly before the operation.

3 It is stated in H. p. 31 that the task organisation is shown in Annex A of the Operation plan, but it is not contained in the copy supplied to the Admiralty.

The Naval Forces engaged in the Assault were:[1]

5	Battleships	(3 U.S., 1 British, 1 French)
17	Cruisers	(6 U.S., 6 British, 5 French)
4	A/A Cruisers	British
9	Escort Carriers	(2 U.S., 7 British)
87	Destroyers	(54 U.S., 26 British, 3 French, 4 Greek)
2	Corvettes	British
2	Gunboats	British
25	P.C.	U.S.
29	S.C.	U.S.
35	Minesweepers	(13 U.S., 22 British)
32	Y.M.S.	(26 U.S., 6 British)
27	M.L.	British
6	Danlayers	British
3	Auxiliary Minelayers and minesweeping depot ships	(2 U.S., 1 British)
4	Fighter Defence Ships and Trawlers	British
4	H.Q. ships	U.S.
19	Combat Loaders	U.S.
9	Transports	U.S.
10	L.S.I.	British
1	L.S.P.	British
1	Repair Ship	U.S.
2	L.S.D.	British
2	L.S.G.	British
1	L.S.C.	British
3	Tankers	French
21	Tugs	(15 U.S., 6 British)
4	Salvage Vessels	British
1	Netlayer	U.S.
6	Motor Fishing Vessels	British vessels, French crews
81	L.S.T.	(75 U.S., 3 British, 3 Greek)
124	L.C.I.	(97 U.S., 27 British)
142	L.C.T.	(77 U.S., 65 British)
30	L.C.T.(R)	British but 14 had American crews
6	L.C.F.	British
5	L.C.G.	British
42	P.T. boats	U.S.
17	Air Sea Rescue Craft	(16 U.S., 1 British)
63	Cargo Ships	

1 H. p. 30.

Thus in all 881 ships and major landing craft took part in the assault in addition to which about 1,370 smaller craft were ship-borne or towed to the assault area, making a total force of 2,250 ships and craft.[1]

9. The Naval Assault Plan

Some aspects of the naval plan have already been dealt with and it now remains to deal broadly with the assault plan. The "Sitka" Support Force was to arrive at a position about 25 miles south of Cape Camarat at 2150 on 14th August, and by 2300 two groups of landing ships were to have taken up their positions off the Islands of Port Cros and Levant, while the third group containing the French Commandos, was to lie further off shore near the support force. Landings from the L.S.I. and from the American destroyer transports were to be effected by L.C.A., L.C.P.(R), L.C.R.[2] and Kayaks, followed by L.C.M. with supplies. The entire force was to be protected by screens of P.T. boats. About 800 French Commandos were to land near Cape Nègre. Of the American forces, 1,400 were to land on Levant Island for the purpose of capturing batteries, while 700 men were to assault Port Cros Island. The landings were to be made by stealth, without preliminary bombardment, at 0130 on 15th August, advance units having been put ashore an hour earlier to mark beaches and the cliffs, which would have to be scaled. Naval bombardment and aerial bombing would be provided, if necessary, minesweepers were to clear the area, and a net tender would remove the net believed to run from Port Cros to Cape Benat.

"Alpha" Assault Force had the duty of establishing ashore the 3rd division over Red beach in Cavalaire Bay and Yellow beach in Parnpelonne Bay. The area was believed to be strongly defended and heavy bombing attacks were to be made from 0550 to 0730.[3] The naval bombardment was to commence at 0700, but might open earlier if enemy batteries were firing, and cease at 0750. Minesweepers, covered by destroyers, were to start clearing the outer area at 0440, and shallow draught vessels were to sweep the inshore areas between 0710 and 0745, while underwater obstacles were to be cleared by drone boats. The boat waves would be covered until 0758 by the fire of L.C.G., L.C.T.(R) and L.C.S., and at 0745 a smoke screen would be put up. The first wave of assaulting infantry with a few tanks and anti-tank guns was to land at 0800. An inner transport area for L.S.T., L.C.I. and L.C.T. was to be laid out five miles to seaward of each beach and outer transport areas for combat loaders and cargo ships a further five miles out to sea. Boat lanes ran between the two areas and from the inner areas to the beaches. L.C.T. and L.C.I. were to beach as soon as possible followed by the L.S.T., which would probably require pontoons. The troops were to strike north, overrun the St. Tropez peninsula, capture Cogolin, and in conjunction with the 45th division secure the roads round Grimaud, and also to push to the west and join hands with the French Commandos ("Romeo" Force). As soon as it was seen that the assault was successful, most of the L.C.T.(R) were to be released to the "Camel" Attack Force Commander for the afternoon assault on Red and Yellow beaches. An assault commander embarked in an L.C.I. was responsible for the attack on each beach and under him three sector commanders, each in an L.C.C., had the duty of controlling traffic, smoke laying, and inshore supporting gunfire.

1 H. p. 133.

2 L.C.R. had previously meant Landing Craft Rocket, but in August 1944, it meant Landing Craft Rubber.

3 H. p. 184, but on p. 253 it is stated that bombing was to be carried out from 0610 to 0730.

The task of the "Delta" Assault Force was to land and maintain the 45th division over beaches in Bougnon Bay. The four beaches, Red, Green, Yellow and Blue, were close together. The ideal landing place would have been the beaches in the Gulf of St. Tropez, but it would have been impossible for minesweepers to clear the gulf before the assault in the face of converging gunfire from the three sides whereas it was believed that the beaches selected had few if any defences, though the area in general was strongly fortified. Aerial bombing was to be carried out from 0550 to 0730, and battleships, cruisers and destroyers would bombard from 0650. Close support fire for the assault boat wave would be given from 0745 to 0756 and smoke would be used if necessary.

The seaward areas were to be cleared by mine sweepers and demolition units were to be used inshore if necessary. The assault troops were to be landed over all four beaches at 0800, and were to push inland as quickly as possible as the small Delta area required a deep bridgehead to prevent the enemy guns from covering the unloading. At the same time troops were to push west in order to open up the Gulf of St. Tropez where the two small ports of St. Tropez and St. Maxime, the good beaches and the excellent anchorage provided far greater facilities for army maintenance than the Bougnon Bay beaches. On the right flank the 45th division was to join troops in the "Camel" Area in the Argens valley and on the left flank it was to make contact with the 3rd division near Grimaud. The northern half of "Alpha" Yellow beach was to be taken over by "Delta" force at noon if the Bougnon Bay beaches were becoming congested. The inner transport area was 7½ miles from the beaches and the outer area another 2½ miles to seaward, with a single swept boat lane serving both areas and branching into four, 1½ miles from the beaches.

10.

"Camel" Assault Force was to land and maintain the 36th Division over four rather widely separated beaches; Red beach in the Gulf of Fréjus near St. Raphael, Green beach near Cape Drammont, Yellow at the end of the Rade d'Agay, and Blue beach at Anthéor Plage. Of these only Green and Blue beaches were to be used for the assault, as Red beach was believed to be too heavily defended and the approach to Yellow beach too well mined, but it was planned to assault Red beach in the afternoon when more support fire and air cover would be available and to capture Yellow beach from landward. Before the assault a commando force was to be landed by the Special Operations Group in darkness in the Gulf of la Napoule to protect the right flank. The outer transport area was twelve miles to seaward of Red beach and was flanked by two small craft reassembly areas; Red and Green beaches were to be served by a common lowering area seven miles from the shore while for Blue beach there was a lowering area 4½ miles out to sea. As in the other sectors boat lanes were to be swept in to the beaches and the seaward areas would be cleared by sweepers. Bombing and naval bombardments were to be carried out as in the other sectors and close support fire would be afforded immediately before the landing which, as in the other areas, was to take place at 0800.

All Combat loaders and L.S.I. were to sail from the area as soon as possible after the assault followed by the L.S.T. and L.C.I., and all convoy destroyer escorts were to be released as soon as their duties were completed, to be detailed for anti-submarine patrols and as escorts of returning convoys. In "Alpha" area the Le Lavandou beaches were to be opened up as soon as possible so as to increase the facilities for the maintenance of the 3rd

Division, and it was hoped to open the three small ports of St. Tropez, St. Maxime and St. Raphael before the close of D-day. Arrangements had been made for the four gunfire support groups to retire for the night into specified areas out to sea. It was laid down that after the assault Admiral Hewitt would put into effect a new organisation whereby only units necessary for the maintenance and build up of the beach heads would remain under the orders of the assault force commanders, the remainder being released and given new tasks by Admiral Hewitt's staff.

Arrangements had been made for the reception and unloading of the first follow up convoys. Of these SM.2, a storeship convoy from Naples, was due to arrive at 1600 on 15th August, at which hour special convoy No. 2, containing French armoured forces from Oran was also scheduled to arrive. Convoy AM.1 consisting of store ships, and L.S.T. from Oran was expected at 1800 on D-day. On 16th August convoys T.F.1 and T.M.1 were due to arrive from Taranto. The first of these was a personnel convoy transporting the 1st French Infantry Division and the 3rd Algerian Infantry Division while the other convoy contained stores and equipment for these troops. It was of the utmost importance that the follow up should be effected rapidly in order that a wide beach-head might be occupied before the enemy could commence any counter-attacks. By the close of 16th August it was hoped that the 6th Corps would have advanced as far as the "Blue Line" (*see Plan* 1), which starting at the Gulf of la Napoule followed roughly the main St. Raphael–Toulon road and railway as far as Le Luc, and then turned south reaching the sea between Hyères and Cape Benat. It may be said that this line was duly reached and in many cases passed before the end of the day.

11. Air Plan

The Allied Air force employed consisted of 84 squadrons of heavy day bombers, 4 squadrons of heavy night bombers, and 6 squadrons of medium night bombers of the Mediterranean Strategical Air Force, about 1,800 aircraft, but these squadrons were not exclusively employed in operation "Dragoon." From the Mediterranean Tactical Air Force 35 squadrons of fighters and fighter bombers were employed, as well as 28 squadrons of medium bombers and 30 squadrons of troop-carriers, night fighters, reconnaissance aircraft and anti-submarine and anti-shipping elements, in all some 1,700 machines. In addition there were about 220 aircraft from the carrier force, and air escorts for the convoys were supplied by the Mediterranean Coastal Air Force to a strength of nearly 300 aircraft.[1]

The strategical forces carried out heavy bombing on objectives in Southern France from 29th April until four hours before the assault. The principal task was to destroy all the bridges over the Rhône from Avignon to the mouth of the river, over the River Durance from Sisteron to its junction with the Rhône, and also the bridges over the Var from its mouth to Annot. All road junctions between the Durance and the Var north of the assault area were to be attacked, as also were tunnels, viaducts, marshalling yards and airfields. In short, the whole assault area was to be isolated. This bombing plan had to be integrated with the general bombing plan for Western Europe in such a way as to disguise the isolation of the assault area. In all 5,408 sorties were flown by the Strategical Air Force, and 6,704 tons of bombs dropped with such success that with one exception every bridge

1 F.80296 071900 August from General Wilson, and operation Plan Annex F Appendix 1, p. 2.

across the Rhône, Durance and Var leading into the assault area was destroyed, while the damage done to roads and railways contributed materially to the enemy's inability to concentrate his forces swiftly after the landings.[1]

The tactical bombing was intended mainly to neutralise the coast defences and radar stations and was to continue from 5th August to 14th August. To prevent the enemy from deducing the exact point of the assault, heavy attacks were directed against the Cette, Marseilles and Genoa areas as well as against the "Dragoon" area. In addition it was planned to carry out intensive bombing immediately before the assault. For this purpose more than 1,300 aircraft were concentrated to carry out attacks against the forty miles of coast line which comprised the assault area. Attacks were to be made on batteries, light artillery positions, airfields, beaches, and military concentrations. These attacks were to be concentrated into eighty minutes[2] and were to cease at 0730, half an hour before the assault. Admiral Hewitt says that the execution of this plan exceeded expectations,[3] in spite of the fact that bad visibility prevented the bombing of some targets.

After the assault, bombing of enemy communications was to continue, but the principal task of the air forces would be the provision of fighter cover over the beaches and transport areas. Fighter direction was assigned to the Commanding General 64th wing, who became Air Defence Commander, and was embarked in the British Fighter Direction Tender 13, a converted L.S.T. *The Ulster Queen* was first standby fighter direction ship, and the *Catoctin* was second standby and, in addition, control ship for offensive fighter bombers. L.S.T.*32*, *140*, and *394* which were specially equipped and furnished with radar were to provide information on aircraft movements during daylight and control night fighters during the dark hours. Four fighter patrols were to be provided giving low, medium and high cover with a total number of aircraft on patrol varying from 28 to 32. Air spotting for naval bombardments was to be carried out by special aircraft of the tactical force, by machines from the carriers and also by aircraft carried in the American cruisers. Other aircraft were detailed for mine spotting. Air-sea rescue operations were to be controlled by H.M.S. *Antwerp*, the ship being stationed half-way between Corsica and the assault area; twelve launches and four pinnaces were detailed for rescue work as well as 23 aircraft. The Army plan and forces employed have already been sufficiently described in Section 1.

12. Topography, Beaches, Enemy Defences. Weather[4]

(*See Plan* 1).

Very thorough air reconnaissance of the assault area was carried out during the months which preceded the landing, and much information was also obtained from the Resistance Movement, as a result of which intelligence was very complete and there were few surprises. The assault area may be considered as extending from Cape Benat on the west to La Napoule, near Cannes, on the east. In general the coast line of the area is not favourable for amphibious operations, having inadequate communications. The beaches are not very good; they are separated by cliffs and rocky shores and can often be enfiladed

1 H. p. 246.
2 H. p. 253 says from 0610 to 0730 but on p. 184 it is stated that bombing was to start at 0550.
3 H. p. 254.
4 The principal source for this section is Annex A to Admiral Hewitt's operation plan, but the Mediterranean Pilot Vol. 2, and B.R. 503, the Geographical Handbook on France, Vols. 1 and 4, have also been consulted.

because of the configuration of the coast. The principal capes, which divide the beaches, are Cape Nègre, the great headland between Cavalaire Bay and the Gulf of St. Tropez which includes Cape Lardier, Cape Camarat and Cape St. Tropez, Issambre Point, Cape Drammont, and Cape Roux. The coast line is cut by some small streams and by the River Argens, which was of great importance for up the valley of this river were to rush the assaulting armoured units the rapid advance of which was essential if the beach head was to be quickly conquered.

The terrain inland consists of a low mountainous region cut by many ravines and extending from the rocky coast to the foothills of the Alps. The hills usually arise directly behind the beaches, but there are small cultivated plains in which villages are situated. The mountains have an arid aspect in summer because of the thin soil, sparse vegetation and high evaporation, and there are large areas of barren rock. During the summer the wooded areas are very dry and there is considerable danger of fire. The drainage is good owing to the slope of the terrain and the porous nature of the soil. A first class road runs from Cannes along the coast to St. Raphael, where it is joined by a secondary road from Cannes which skirts the inland side of the Esterel mountains. From St. Raphael a good coast road runs as far as St. Tropez from which it runs inland to Hyères, Toulon and Marseilles, but a secondary road from St. Tropez cuts across to Cavalaire Bay, follows the coast as far as Le Lavandou and then turns inland to join the Cannes-Hyères road near Bormes. From St. Raphael another first class road runs up the Argens Valley through Fréjus, and Le Muy, traversing the country where the airborne division was to land, and continuing through Le Luc and Carnoules to Hyères, Toulon and Marseilles. From Le Luc a road runs through Brignoles to Aix-en-Provence where it joins the great Paris-Lyon-Marseilles trunk road.

With the exception of the St. Raphael-Le Luc road there is no road of any importance running directly inland from the coast. The main railway line from the Italian frontier skirts the coast as far as St. Raphael and follows the road through Fréjus, Le Luc, Les Arcs, Carnoules and Sollies Ville to Toulon, Marseilles and Paris. From a junction near Sollies Ville a single line runs to Hyères and terminates at Les Salins on the shores of the Gulf of Hyères. From St. Raphael there is a narrow gauge line which follows the coast to St. Tropez, cuts across to Cavalaire Bay, continues along the coast again as far as Le Lavandou and thence runs inland to Hyères and Toulon. A single line runs north from Les Arcs to Draguignan and from Carnoules another single line runs through Brignoles to Marseilles. The only islands off the coast are the Hyères group in the gulf of that name and consisting of Port Cros, Levant, and Porquerolles and the islet of Bagueau. The two first of these were of cardinal importance as their batteries commanded the Cavalaire beach and the entire Alpha transport and fire support areas. These islands were to be captured by Commandos before the main landing, after which operations would be carried out against Porquerolles.

The small ports of St. Raphael, St. Maxime, and St. Tropez, which are in the assault area, were expected to be of great value, though it was known that the Germans had carried out demolitions. St. Raphael could accommodate one vessel of 3,000 tons. The other two ports are smaller, but vessels drawing up to- thirteen feet can enter St. Tropez, and St. Maxime can take ships drawing up to ten feet. But the principal value of these ports was the protection they would afford to small craft and the fact that they could be extensively used by landing craft.

13.

The beach at Le Lavandou was suitable for assault craft, but L.S.T. would have to use pontoons. The beach extends over 1,800 yards and after some preparation of exits would be suitable for landing tanks. This beach was not scheduled to be assaulted, but was to be opened up as soon as possible for landing troops from the follow up convoys. The three beaches between Le Lavandou and Cape Nègre, covering in all 2,350 yards but separated by small rocky promontories, have easy gradients and were considered to be suitable for all types of landing craft up to and including L.S.T., which it was thought would not need pontoons. These beaches like that at Le Lavandou were to be opened up as soon as possible after the assault. Just to the east of Cape Nègre is a beach on which a small French commando force was to land, while the remainder of the French commandos were to land on a beach a mile and a half to the eastward.

These two beaches and another between them were too small to be of much use for maintenance. "Alpha" Red beach, which was in Cavalaire Bay and extended over 3,900 yards, was a good beach from the naval point of view in spite of a sand bar lying off it. It could be used by all types of landing craft though it was thought that in some places landings would be wet, and that L.S.T. would require pontoons in the centre part of the beach though not in the east and west sectors. The beach exits were fairly good and the army considered that the beach would be suitable for maintenance. This beach was prolonged by another stretch of sand 1,500 yards long, the exits from which were poor and which was not to be used for the assault though it was thought that it might be opened after a thorough survey. "Alpha" Yellow beach was in Pampelonne Bay, separated from Red beach by the Lardier-Camarat headland. This was a fine beach 4,500 yards long with good exits. The sand bars off the beach were not expected to impede most landing craft but a survey would be necessary before sending in L.S.T. and large L.C.T.

The four "Delta" beaches, Red, Green, Yellow and Blue were situated between Cape Sardineau and Issambre Point. The first three were really part of the same beach, in all some 800 yards long. It was doubtful if L.S.T. could use these beaches without pontoons, and their bad exits reduced their utility from the army point of view, but they were only to be used for the assault, the follow up being made through St. Tropez and Ste. Maxime. Blue beach was about a mile to the N.E., it was suitable for all types of landing craft but had no exits. The Camel Red Beach was in the Gulf of Fréjus immediately to the S.W. of the town of St. Raphael; it is 2,700 yards long and though obstructed in places by a sand bar it was thought that landing craft could easily make the beach. It was considered that L.S.T. would be able to beach in many places and other craft anywhere on the beach; exits were good and the army pronounced the beach suitable for maintenance.

"Camel" Green beach was immediately to the west of Cape Drammont and was 840 yards long, the gradients making it suitable for all types of landing craft up to and including L.S.T. but the exits were only fair and its use to the army after the assault would be limited. Yellow beach was at the head of the Rade d'Agay; it is 1,100 yards in length and was thought to be suitable for L.S.T.; beach exits again were poor. Blue beach was situated at Anthéor Plage about two miles east of Yellow beach and separated from it by a headland; it is a small beach only 80 yards long and though suitable for small craft it was unlikely that L.C.T. or L.S.T. could use it owing to lack of space for manoeuvring. The American Commandos were to land on Levant Island at a very small beach in the Anse du Liserot and at four other places where there was no beach, and on Port Cros Island the raiding party was to avoid the beaches possibly because they were considered to be too far from the objective. On the extreme right flank French Commandos were to be landed at Pointe des Deux Frères near Théoule-sur-Mer.

14.

The Riviera was very strongly defended by coast defence batteries. Between Marseilles and Nice there were 199 batteries mounting 647 guns. The defences of the assault area were comparatively weak but even so they totalled 29 batteries mounting 88 guns of three-inch calibre and above, as well as 34 casemates, some of which were not occupied.[1] The heaviest batteries were, firstly one of three 6.5-inch guns on the N.E. point of Levant Island;[2] a battery of five 8.8-inch guns was situated on Cape St. Tropez.[3] Near Agay there was a battery of five 6-inch guns, but it was not certain whether it was completed, and finally, on Issambre Point there were three 8.8 inch guns with three dummy guns near by. Of guns below three inch and machine-guns, there were large numbers often in concrete emplacements and pill boxes. Most of the beaches were defended by mined obstacles of different types and some by shallow water mines. Owing to the absence of tide these were never uncovered and it would be a matter of some difficulty to clear them, but on the other hand they were more difficult to erect than would have been the case in tidal waters. With regard to deep sea mines, the hundred fathom line was so near the coast of the assault area in most places (from three to six miles) that the zone of mineable water was very restricted. Not much was known about the enemy's deep sea minefields. Submarines had been used for reconnaissance but without much success, and a well laid field of 90 mines in the Gulf of Fréjus was a surprise, as on July 28th a submarine had reported that no mines could be detected.[4] On the other hand a minefield reported at the mouth of the Gulf of St. Tropez did not exist.[5]

The weather was confidently expected to be favourable for the assault and to continue good till the end of the month; in September occasional strong off shore winds were probable, but there was no expectation of a "mistral" until the end of September. It had been realised during the planning that beach maintenance would be impossible in October, and that it would be necessary to open up a big port before then. In point of fact both Toulon and Marseilles were captured on 28th August, and though unloading over the beaches continued after this date, weather only interfered with unloading on one occasion, on 3rd September.[6] Sunrise On 15th August was at 0639 and sunset at 2035.

15. The Enemy Forces

The naval forces of the enemy in the Western Mediterranean on July 24th were insignificant. They consisted of one destroyer,[7] five torpedo boats, the equivalent of our Hunt class, seven escort vessels of corvette type, five of the so called "heavily armed

1 H. p. 139.
2 This battery turned out to be a dummy.
3 After the assault it was found that in reality these guns were 6.5 inch.
4 H. p. 144.
5 H. p. 144.
6 H. p. 136.
7 Operation Plan Annex A.

vessels" which were small armed merchant ships used as escorts, fifteen[1] M.A.S. boats (Italian M.T.Bs.), fifteen minesweepers, twenty-five miscellaneous auxiliaries and five or six submarines active, plus several damaged in air raids on Toulon. These ships were based at different ports along the coast from Marseilles to Genoa. In addition there were two destroyers refitting at Genoa which it was thought might soon be in commission. Of these vessels one destroyer,[2] one torpedo boat, thirteen escort vessels,[3] three minesweepers and five submarines were destroyed during the operation.

A greater threat than these war vessels was perhaps the human torpedoes, explosive boats with remote control, and limpeteers, though in point of fact they were of little use to the enemy. Sixteen explosive boats and thirteen human torpedoes were destroyed during the course of the operations. A far greater potential menace to the invasion forces was the Luftwaffe. It was estimated that the enemy had based within easy range of the assault area on 25th July[4] 175 torpedo bombers, twenty-five single engine fighters, ten twin engine fighters and thirty reconnaissance machines. There were another 800 fighters in Northern France and Italy and 170 heavy bombers in Northern France, but the extent to which these forces could be used to reinforce the South of France would depend on operations in these two theatres. The greatest threat from the Luftwaffe was the different types of controlled missiles which had inflicted heavy losses on the Allied naval forces during the Salerno and Anzio operations, but by August 1944 considerable strides had been made in coping with these new weapons. In the event the German Air Force was not able to interfere with our operations and no major vessel was damaged by air attack.

Opposed to our assault forces was the German 19th Army under General von Blaskowitz. This Army had once had a strength of thirteen divisions, but reinforcements had been sent to Normandy and on July 28th it was estimated to be composed of six infantry divisions,[5] not all at full strength, and one armoured division. Early in August another armoured division appeared to be moving from Bordeaux towards the Mediterranean coast while an infantry division was due to arrive from the Pyrenees. Last minute information was to the effect that the armoured division from Bordeaux had stopped near Toulouse while the 11th Panzer Division in Provence had started to move northwards. In addition there were a considerable number of miscellaneous troops, mostly of poor quality. In the assault area was stationed the 242nd Infantry Division but it was thought that three days after the assault the enemy might concentrate three to four divisions, including possibly one armoured division.

16. Preparations, Training, Rehearsals

A combined training centre was opened at Salerno as early as February because it was realised that most of the assault divisions would be withdrawn from the Italian front, and it was desired to avoid waste of time in transporting troops to North Africa for training and back to the Naples area for embarkation, while owing to the shorter distance from the assault area, it was necessary to mount most of the expedition at Naples. In the event

1 In H. p. 35 the number of M.A.S. boats on 9th August is given as 30 which figure presumably included the minesweepers, the number of heavily armed vessels as 6, and the number of submarines as 3. Some of the M.A.S. boats were in reality German S. boats which are very similar.

2 H. p. 133.

3 This presumably includes the corvettes and the heavily armed vessels

4 Operation Plan Annex A.

5 Operation Plan Annex A and C.O.S.(44)713(0) of 9th August.

the time factor was even more important than had been anticipated owing to the late date at which it was possible to withdraw the American divisions from the fighting line; moreover, all three divisions were taken from the Italian front.

Every effort was made to reproduce enemy defensive methods and obstacles on the Salerno beaches, and before any troops were available for training many experiments had been carried out to discover methods of breaching underwater obstacles and beach defences. The 45th Division arrived at Salerno and began training on 24th June and the 36th Division commenced on 8th July. The 3rd Division trained at Pozzuoli, a little to the north of Naples, commencing on 6th July. Late in June, 28 L.S.T. and 19 L.C.T. arrived from the United States followed a month later by a force of P.C. and Y.M.S. Late in July there arrived the assault shipping released from Normandy by General Eisenhower and consisting of six combat loaders, 24 L.C.I. and 24 L.C.T., followed by a number of mine-sweepers and by a strong force of rocket craft (L.C.T. (R.)).

The naval reinforcements for the bombarding squadrons mostly arrived from the United Kingdom late in July or early in August; in some cases the margin of time was very small, for instance the *Ramillies* only arrived at Algiers on 11th August so that instead of sailing from Malta with the "Alpha" gunfire support group, she had to rendezvous with it early on D-day. During the training period all three divisions practised landings by day and night from L.S.T., L.C.I., and L.C.T., and ship to shore exercises from a combat loader were also carried out. The commandos trained at Agropoli with four American destroyer transports (A.P.D.) which on 4th August were joined by four L.S.I., one more A.P.D. and nine P.T. boats; on 7th August they carried out a full scale rehearsal on Ponza Island. Gunfire support ships carried out a three day bombardment exercise at the Camerota range and communication practices were carried out to ensure smooth co-ordination between the bombarding ships, spotting aircraft and shore fire control parties. The 3rd Division carried out a full scale landing rehearsal on July 31st in the Gulf of Gaeta during which 146 ships and craft were employed, and some days later the other two divisions did the same, landing over the Salerno beaches in co-operation with all the Air Forces. So life-like were these rehearsals that practically no change in organisation or procedure had to be made.[1]

17. The Convoys sail. Passage

On 9th August Admiral Hewitt by signal[2] ordered his operation plan to be put into effect and announced D-day as August 15th and H-hour as 0800.

On 11th August the C.-in-C. Mediterranean set up an advanced command post at Ajaccio in H.M.S. *Largs*. The first of the convoys to sail was SS1, 1A and 1B, composed mainly of L.C.T. which departed from Naples at 1000 on August 9th. The L.C.I. and L.S.T. convoys sailed from the Naples area on 12th August and the remainder also put to sea according to schedule as shown in *Appendices* C and D. Convoy AM1 consisting of store and ammunition ships sailed from Oran on 10th August, and next day special convoy No. 2, containing the French Armoured Brigade ("Combat Command Sudre") also sailed from Oran, while from Taranto the merchant ship convoy TM1 sailed on 10th August. All convoys sailed without incident. The fact that the great agglomeration of

1 H. p. 168.
2 090930 and 091750 August.

ships and craft in the Gulf of Naples had failed to provoke any air attack from the enemy was an index of the decline of the Luftwaffe. No attacks from submarines or aircraft were made on the convoys during their passage though they were sighted several times by the enemy's reconnaissance aircraft, so the vigilance of our air and surface escorts was not tested. Various ships joined and left convoys during the passage according to the operation plan. As arranged, the SS1 and SF2 convoys staged at Ajaccio while convoy SY1 staged at Propriano. The weather was perfect during the passage, and the few L.C.T. which straggled from their convoys had no difficulty in rejoining at Ajaccio.

18. The Approach

On 14th August the C.-in-C. Mediterranean who was in H.M.S. *Kimberly* watching the progress of the assault convoys through the Straits of Bonifacio, made the signal "carry out Operation Dragoon."[1] At this juncture the Commando Convoy (SY1) was, only some 30 miles from its objective, the L.C.T. convoys had long passed points AL AM and AN and were well up the approach corridors, which the L.S.T. convoys had just entered; the L.C.I. convoys had just sailed from Ajaccio while the convoys of combat loaders and L.S.I. had been joined by their gunfire support groups[2] and would arrive at the entrance to the approach corridors in under two hours. All rendezvous were made in accordance with the operation plan. The approach lanes had been fixed so as to give the minimum period of contact to the enemy's radar, to give as much sea room as possible for manoeuvring the large forces involved, and to keep the assault convoys well clear of the carrier force. The assault convoys were released to the Task Force Commanders as soon as they entered the lanes. The reference Vessels (mark boats) which were mostly P.C. and S.C. were detached to take up their assigned stations.

As the "Camel" convoys had to make a turn to port of eleven degrees from the end of the corridor to the transport area, a destroyer was stationed at the turning point, while a second destroyer marked the right flank of the "Camel" transport area. The minesweepers were detached at 0300 on 15th August to execute their tasks and the gunfire support ships proceeded to their positions for the bombardment which was to commence at 0650. All the convoys arrived in the transport areas punctually and according to plan and the anti-submarine surface patrols were put into effect. Everything had gone according to schedule except for the fact that the "Alpha" combat loader convoy passed through the slower L.C.I. convoy off Ajaccio at dusk on 14th August. This was caused by the having sailed from Ajaccio an hour early, while the other convoy was half an hour behind schedule.[3] Fortunately no serious consequences attended this untoward encounter.

The slow speed of the L.C.T. convoys had caused considerable concern during planning but these convoys all arrived safely in the assault area at the specified time. The Carrier Force arrived in its operating area at about 0530 and the first aircraft was flown off at 0610. The "Sitka" Force encountered the enemy auxiliary *Escaburt* escorted by the *Camoscio* to the south-west of Port Cros Island and U.S.S. *Somers* promptly sank both of them at 0500, while five small enemy patrol craft were destroyed by the "Alpha" minesweepers in Pampelonne Bay at about the same time. Shore based fighters began

1 C.-in-C. Med. 141818 August.
2 "Alpha" gunfire support group did not- rendezvous with the assault convoy but proceeded independently.
3 H. p. 175.

reporting to the Fighter Direction Ship at 0550 and the first patrol arrived at 0615. These fighter patrols dropped bombs on previously assigned targets before reporting for defence and patrol duties. Heavy and medium bombers commenced intensive bombing attacks on the beaches and at 0650 the guns of the battleships, cruisers and destroyers opened a heavy fire. The assault had commenced.

II

THE ASSAULT

19. "Sitka" Sector

The "Sitka" Support Force (T.F. 86) consisting of the cruisers *Augusta,* flagship of Rear-Admiral Davidson, and *Dido,* with the destroyers *Somers, Cleaves* and *Lookout,* arrived at a point 25 miles south of Cape Camarat shortly before 2200 on 14th August. About an hour later two groups of transports and L.S.I. carrying the American Commandos arrived off the Islands of Port Cros and Levant, while the third group transportingthe French Commandos took up its position near the Support Force. At 0030 on 15th August advance scouts and preparatory units were landed on the two islands and on Cape Nègre unobserved by the enemy. In this sector the plan called for a landing by stealth without previous minesweeping and without support of naval guns though the cruisers and destroyers could be called upon if necessary for bombardment after the landing.

The French Commandos embarked in the small craft and at 0130 one party of 75 men was landed at Cape Nègre, but the westerly set of the current and haze on the water caused the second party of 750 troops to land on a beach some two miles to the west of the intended point. This made little difference for there was small opposition from the enemy and once the beach-head was established L.C.M. were sent in with supplies. At 0742 the French complained that they were being bombed by allied aircraft, but by 1000 they had carried out their task of destroying the enemy defences on Cape Nègre, seized the high ground two miles north of the Cape, and blocked the coastal highway thus protecting the left flank of the main assault. Enemy resistance was nowhere serious and the French casualties were light; the Germans made one counterattack but this was repulsed with the help of gunfire from the *Augusta, Dido* and *Ajax* and later in the day the French made contact with the American 3rd Division of "Alpha" Attack Force. Meanwhile, at 0130 the American Commandos landed from their L.C.A., L.C.P.(R), L.C.R., and kayaks. A force of 1,400 men was landed on Levant Island, and 700 on Port Gros without opposition from the enemy. By 0920 the initial resistance on the islands had been overcome; the heavy battery on Levant Island was captured but proved to be a dummy, and a number of prisoners were taken, but isolated strong points still held out and not until 2234 did resistance on Levant Island cease while a party of the enemy still resisted in the old fort at Port Cros and prevented L.S.T.*32* from entering the port and landing radar equipment for a fighter direction station which was to have been set up ashore.

The transports sailed early for Ajaccio leaving two behind to evacuate casualties and prisoners, and one of these sailed at 1600. Casualties to the American forces were very light and no naval craft was damaged except one L.C.A. which sustained a hit from an 88 mm. shell at Port Cros. It is interesting to notice that it was found that the British L.C.A. was superior to the American L.C.P.(R) for these surprise landings on rocky shores, as it was easier to manoeuvre and less noisy. At daylight minesweeping commenced. The

British 5th Minesweeping Flotilla assisted by four M.Ls. was responsible for sweeping channels into the islands and the waters to the south and east of them inside the hundred fathom line; the fire support areas were also swept and an east-west channel north of the islands was to be cleared. These tasks were all duly carried out by 17th August but no mines were swept in the "Sitka" area except between Cape Benat and Port Cros where 36 mines were dealt with by the sweepers and M.Ls. often under fire from a battery on the cape. During these operations M.L.559 was damaged by a mine and the danlayer *Kintyre* was hit by a shell.[1]

It had been thought that there was a net between Port Cros and Cape Benat and a net tender was present to remove it, but it was found that there was no such obstruction. However, Rear-Admiral Davidson thinks the net may have been sunk below the surface and that this may have been the cause of the difficulties and loss of gear experienced by the sweepers when they subsequently tried to force an entrance into the Hyères Roads.[2]

At 0700 the French battleship *Lorraine* arrived to join the Support Force but she was not required and sailed for Propriano in the afternoon to stand by. Little gunfire support was required by the troops on Levant Island though at 0807 the Lookout fired 33 rounds at some enemy troops on the west of the Island,[3] but considerable bombardment was required to reduce Port Cros, where the *Augusta* fired 281 rounds of 8-inch before the final surrender of the fort on 17th August, supported by the *Somers* 692 rounds, and finally on 17th August by the *Ramillies* which arrived from "Alpha" sector and fired twelve rounds of 15-in at the fort and brought about the final collapse of the defence, after which the battleship sailed for Propriano where she remained on call. The bombardment of the *Ramillies* was spotted by aircraft from the *Quincy* and resulted in six direct hits.[4] The *Dido* and the *Gleaves* carried out bombardments of strong points and batteries between Cape Nègre and Le Lavandou though these were in "Alpha" area, and helped to defeat the German counter-attack on the French Commandos. The *Dido* fired 502 rounds[5] and the destroyer 195. Support in this area was also given by the *Aurora, Ajax, Orion,* and *Quincy* and by the destroyers *Livermore* and *Ericsson* all of which ships belonged to the "Alpha" force.

20. "Alpha" Sector[6]

The "Alpha" assault began at 0300 when the P.C. boats detailed to act as mark boats took station ten miles off Red and Yellow beaches, followed by the stationing of the five mile mark boats. At 0440 minesweeping commenced and by 0630 the British 13th Minesweeping Flotilla, together with four American fleet sweepers and sixteen American Y.M.S. and S.C. boats equipped as shallow sweepers, had swept the gunfire support and transport areas and also the boat lanes up to 1,000 yards from the beaches. No mines were found. In Pampelonne Bay the British sweepers were attacked by five small enemy

1 M09992/45. R. of P. S.O. 5th MIS Flotilla p. 2. Admiral Hewitt's report p. 211 says that no mines were swept in the "Sitka" area, but most of these inines were on the dividing line between Sitka and Alpha.

2 M09992/45 Admiral Davidson's covering letter p.

3 There is little information about bombardments in the narrative of Admiral Hewitt's report, but diagrams 18 to 23 at the end of the report give full details.

4 M0115 /44 R. of P. Ramillies Part 1 p. 4.

5 MO11533 R. of P. Dido. The figures given in H. diagram 18 are slightly different.

6 Information about the "Alpha" Sector is more copious and detailed than that on the other sectors, partly because the bombardment force was mainly British. The details given about the organisation of boat waves for the assault apply equally to the Delta and Camel sectors.

patrol vessels all of which they destroyed without themselves suffering any damage. The sweepers also came under fire from shore batteries which they engaged with their guns. By 0500 the gunfire support, L.S.T., L.C.T., and combat loader convoys had arrived. At 0640 the L.C.I. convoy arrived and with the L.S.T. and L.C.T. moved to the inner transport areas. At 0745 the combat loaders moved in.

From 0710 to 0745 the shallow minesweepers cleared the boat lanes from the point reached by the fleet sweepers to within a hundred yards of the beaches. The gunfire support ships fired at the allotted targets from 0700 to 0750. The drone boats were sent in from 0710 to 0730, nine to each beach. All the drones on Red beach detonated as planned except that they were concentrated too much on the left side of the beach but on Yellow beach three failed to function properly and one of these exploded prematurely and severely damaged S.C.1029, one of the mark boats. From 0750 to 0758 the L.C.T. (R) six at Red beach and four at Yellow, L.C.M.(R) seven craft at each beach and the L.C.S.(S) poured a stream of rockets on to the beaches, while the L.C.G. and L.C.F. fired from close inshore. Combined with the off-shore bombardment and the aerial bombing the result was "an overwhelming concerted blow of only one hour and fifty minutes duration which dazed and weakened the enemy; and the Army was placed ashore with extremely light losses".[1]

The firing of the rockets was arranged in successive waves of barrages which must have upset any idea of the enemy that rocket fire was a one punch weapon.[2] Meanwhile the combat loaders and L.S.I. had lowered their assault craft and the first waves were approaching the shore; some of the boats were endangered by rockets which dropped short. The enemy's gunfire was light and was limited to mortar and machine-gun fire with a few rounds of 88 mm. The first wave of assault craft was the largest. It was composed of the support craft and the first troop wave. The boat minesweepers led by an S.G. or an L.C.C. proceeded first to conduct a sweep of the boat lanes, and where amphibious scouts were used they preceded the initial wave and carried out a rapid hydrographic reconnaissance for obstacles. The drone boats were directed by the L.C.C. and were in the van of the support wave. Deployed astern of them and in the van of the first troop wave were the "Woofus Craft" (L.C.M.(R)), while the rocket firing L.C.S.(S) were stationed between the formations of L.C.V.P. or L.C.A., which were carrying troops, and when ordered by the L.C.C. speeded ahead at firing time. On the flanks of the first wave were the L.C.F. and L.C.G. to render close gunfire support and also some L.C.T. carrying D.D. tanks[3] and tank destroyers.

Each formation of L.C.V.P. was led by an L.C.C. which directed the craft to their assigned beaches, the L.C.T.(R.) followed astern of the L.C.V.P. and fired over them at the beach. Those of the L.C.C. which were not required for immediate control at the beaches returned to the line of departure to assist in guiding in the later waves. The L.C.I. and L.C.T. were usually led in from the transport area by a craft of their own type. The D.U.K.W.S. were guided by L.C.C. or L.C.V.P. and released when about 1000 yards from the beach. In guiding the later waves the L.C.C. were helped by S.C. boats.[4] Two battalions of the 7th R.C.T. and two of the 15th R.C.T. were to land over Red and Yellow

1 H. is. 285.
2 M04531/45 Rear-Admiral Lowry's remarks para. 5.
3 These were the amphibious tanks first used in the Normandy landings.
4 H. pp. 216, 217.

beaches respectively, followed by the 30th R.C.T. and ancillary units over Red beach. The first two waves were to land by divisions of five boats; the assault craft were organised in such a way that a company with three rifle platoons would touch down first at the centre and on each flank while the heavy weapon platoons would land each side of the centre one minute later. For the assault phase there was an assault commander for each beach embarked in a command L.C.I., or in British parlance an L.C.H. Under the assault commander were three sector commanders each in an L.C.C., charged with control of all traffic, smoke laying, and close inshore fire in their respective sectors.[1]

21.

The first assault waves landed with little hindrance at 0800 and were followed by eight other waves which landed on schedule, though the ninth wave on Red beach was delayed by shallow water mines on the right flank of the beach. These waves of assault craft were followed by L.C.T. and L.C.I. Enemy gunfire continued to be innocuous but three L.C.V.P. and four L.C.I. were damaged by teller mines while beaching on the right end of Red beach where no drone boats had exploded. At 1030 the L.S.T. were sent in to place pontoons and at 1045 the Commanding General of the 3rd Division landed and set up his headquarters ashore. Removal of land mines on Red beach caused some delay in unloading as did a shortage of truck drivers and beach labour, but matters were remedied by placing trucks in L.C.M., loading bulk cargo in slings directly from the ships into the trucks and sending the trucks from the L.C.M. to unload directly at the dumps. On Yellow beach all landing craft were unloaded by 1400, though a certain amount of congestion was caused by the narrowness of the exits. At 1545 unloading over the right or eastern half of Red beach had to be stopped until mines could be cleared, but additional landing points were put into use and at 1800 Green Beach, in the eastern corner of Cavalaire Bay, was opened, though the exits were found to be heavily mined. At 1700 all the original assault troops having landed, a reorganisation of the naval forces was put into effect in order to provide for the maintenance and follow up phase.

Ships and craft reported for the assignment of new tasks, and the existing forces with the addition of some P.T. boats for patrolling the western flank were reconstituted into a Screening and Smoke Group, Gunfire Support Group, Minesweeping Group, Salvage and Firerfighting Unit, Area Unloading Control, Joint Loading Control, and Naval Beach Party. After the "Alpha" Assault the L.C.T.(R.) were ordered to proceed to "Camel" sector where they were to be employed in the afternoon assault on Red beach. Only three pontoons had been supplied for "Alpha" area, but it was arranged that nine more should be sent from the other sectors as required. The Gunfire Support Group for "Alpha" sector consisted of the *Ramillies,* the *Orion,* wearing the flag of Rear-Admiral Mansfield, *Aurora, Ajax, Black Prince,* the American Cruiser *Quincy,* the French cruiser *Gloire,* the British destroyers *Terpsichore* and *Termagant* and the American destroyers *Livermore, Eberle, Kearney* and *Ericsson.* Heavy bombardments were carried out by these ships. Before the assault the targets were chiefly coast defence batteries, particularly those commanding Yellow beach, and the beach areas. After the assault, ships were to fire at troop concentrations and other targets as required; but in point of fact there was little firing after 0800 in "Alpha" beach areas as the troops required no support and moved

1 H. p. 185.

rapidly inland, so the ships moved to the westward and engaged targets between Cape Nègre and Cape Benat supported by some of the Sitka ships. Admiral Lowry, who was in command of the "Alpha" assault particularly praises the shooting of the *Aurora,* which silenced a battery near Cape Benat after firing only six rounds.[1] The *Ramillies* fired ten rounds at the heavy battery to the south of St. Tropez at 0615[2] and at 0654 she fired 24 rounds at a battery near Cape Camarat without any reply from the enemy.

Altogether the *Aurora* fired 409 rounds, the *Orion* 40, the *Ajax* 116, the *Black Prince* 80, the *Gloire* 149 and the *Quincy* 143. Of the destroyers the *Livermore* was the most heavily engaged, firing 644 rounds, the *Kearney* 528 the *Ericsson* 267 and the *Eberle* upwards of 200 rounds; some of the destroyers also fired with light weapons.[3] The *Termagant* and *Terpsichore* engaged batteries and strong points near Yellow beach, but their complete figures for ammunition expended are not given. Admiral Lowry comments on the very effective beach neutralising fire carried out by the *Terpsichore, Termagant* and *Ericsson,*[4] the latter using a walking barrage to cover the centre of Yellow beach. Much of the spotting was done by L.C.C. and even by the bombarding ships themselves but the aircraft from the *Quincy* also did very good work. Admiral Mansfield particularly commends the work of the *Quincy* (Captain Senn) and the *Gloire* (Capitaine de Vaisseau Adam).[5] The shore fire control parties were of little use on D-Day as the army advanced so quickly, in some cases as much as thirty miles in the day, that they had difficulty in keeping up, nevertheless the *Terpsichore* established contact with her shore fire control only half an hour after the landing.[6] The only casualty to the bombarding ships was a hit from a 47 mm. shell on the *Livermore* which did little damage.

Of the close support craft, L.C.G.4 and L.C.F.4 were stationed off Red beach and L.C.G.8 and L.C.F.8 off Yellow beach; most of these craft reported that the smoke screens interfered with their fire.[7] The two L.C.G. withdrew to Ajaccio on 16th August followed by the L.C.F. the following day. The fact that the L.C.F. could be dispensed with so early, shows how little apprehension was felt about enemy air attacks.

22. "Delta" Sector

The stationing of the mark boats commenced as early as midnight. Minesweeping was started at 0300 by the British 19th Minesweeping Flotilla reinforced by two American fleet sweepers and a number of M.L.s and Y.M.S.; no mines were swept. The scout boats reported that there were no underwater obstacles protecting the beaches so at 0543 Rear Admiral Rodgers cancelled the orders for the use of drone boats. Meanwhile at 0440 the L.C.T. convoy had arrived in the inner transport area followed by the gunfire support group, while the combat loader and L.S.T. convoys arrived in their transport area at 0500. At 0800 the L.C.I. reached the inner area. The bombardment was particularly important

1 M0107/45 Rear-Admiral Lowry's comments on Rear-Admiral Mansfield's Report para. 29. In point of fact diagram 18 in Admiral Hewitt's Report shows that the Aurora in all fired 72 rounds at this battery between 1057 and 1559. No R. of P. covering D-day has been received from the Aurora.

2 M011587/44 R. of P. Ramillies para. 21. Diagram 18 of H. shows this bombardment as having taken place at 0812, but this diagram is not always accurate.

3 MO107/45 App. I. Figures given here for the British destroyers seem incomplete.

4 MO107/45 Rear-Admiral Lowry's comments paras. 35 to 38.

5 M0107/45 R. of P. Rear-Admiral Mansfield paras. 12 and 13.

6 MO107/45 Rear-Admiral Lowry's comments para. 36.

7 M04531/45 R. of P. Lt.-Cdr. Wilde R.N. S.O. 'F' Support Craft Squadron in L.C.G.4 and reports of individual craft.

in "Delta" sector owing to the strength of the coast defences. It was most effective and by H-hour the air and naval bombardments had put out of action all major guns, and most of the coast defence crews had deserted their posts,[1] with the result that no enemy shells fell in the transport areas and only about 60 rounds of mortar fire and a few rounds of 75 mm. fell in the boat lanes, doing no damage. More than 6,000 rockets were fired at the beach defences, paralysing the enemy, although the L.C.M. (R.) from the *Eastway* did not arrive in time.

The arrangements for the assault and support were similar to the organisation already described for "Alpha" sector. The first waves had landed by 0802 and by 0910 the first seven waves of troops were ashore. The 157th R.C.T. landed over Red and Green beaches and the 180th R.C.T. over Blue and Yellow beaches, followed by the 179th R.C.T. The Commanding General of the 45th Division landed at 1100 and in the afternoon the Commanding General of the 6th Corps disembarked. The L.S.T. had to use pontoons at Red and Green beaches, but on the other two beaches unloading was accomplished dry. All L.C.T., L.C.I. and combat loaders had been emptied of troops and vehicles by 2145 and the unloading of the merchant vessels had started.

A rapid advance of the troops was most necessary in this sector, which was very narrow, so as to prevent enemy mobile guns being set up to cover the unloading, this rapidity was fully achieved and Ste. Maxime was captured by 1700. The amphibious tanks, from which much had been hoped, were not a great success, five out of twelve being stopped by mines on the beach, and two more knocked out, also by mines, soon after. By 1600 all troops had landed and the reorganisation plan was put into effect as in "Alpha" sector. The assault plan had envisaged the possibility of the small "Delta" beaches becoming very congested, in which case it had been determined to use the northern half of "Alpha" Yellow, but this was not necessary, and during the day 11 combat loaders, transport and cargo ships, 30 L.S.T., 41 L.C.T., and 36 L.C.I. were unloaded over the four exiguous beaches giving a total of 33,000 persons and 3,300 vehicles[2] besides quantities of stores. Army losses were very light; there were no naval casualties and no vessel was hit by enemy fire.

The Gunfire Support Group consisted of the American battleships *Texas* and *Nevada,* the cruisers *Philadelphia, Georges Leygues* and *Montcalm,* three French and eight American destroyers. The *Nevada* fired 106 rounds of 14 inch[3] at the heavy coastal battery on Issambre Point during the pre H hour bombardment while the *Texas* during the same period fired 172 rounds at the heavy battery near St. Tropez spotting in both cases being carried out by destroyers inshore. In the afternoon the *Nevada* sailed for Propriano, where she remained on call, while the *Texas* sailed for Algiers on 17th August. The *Philadelphia* was heavily engaged and fired 610 rounds during the day, both before and after the assault, using chiefly her own aircraft for spotting, though the shore fire control party was also at times employed. The *Georges Leygues* fired 290 rounds and the *Montcalm* 246. Of the destroyers the *Rodman* fired 543 rounds, the *Emmons* 434, the *Macomb* 400, the *Hobson* 361, the *Ellyson* 343, and the *Hambleton* 255 rounds, the *Fitch* and the *Forrest* being less heavily engaged; in general the American destroyers did their own spotting. Of the French destroyers the *Fantasque* fired 231 rounds, *Le Terrible* 120, and *Le Malin* 35. As has already been mentioned the naval gunfire was most effective.

1 H. p. 188.
2 H. p. 189.
3 Details of bombardments are taken from diagram 19 of Admiral Hewitt's report

23. "Camel" Sector

In this sector only two of the four beaches, Blue and Green, were to be assaulted at H-hour, as the other two were thought to be too strongly defended. Red beach, in the Gulf of Fréjus, would be attacked in the afternoon at a time to be fixed by the Commanding General of the 36th Division, when rocket craft from the other sectors would be available to augment the fire and when a heavier air bombardment could be provided. The capture of this beach was most important not only for the rapid build up of the division, since Blue beach was extremely small, and Green beach was not thought to be very satisfactory, but also on account of its position at the mouth of the Argens valley up which the French armoured troops were to push as soon as possible, and its proximity to the port of St. Raphael, the airfield at Fréjus and the main coast road and railway. No assault was planned for Yellow beach, at the head of the Rade d'Agay, but it was hoped to capture it from landward before the close of D-day.

The assault opened with the landing of seventy French commandos at Deux Frères Point, south of Théoule, from P.T. boats at 0010. These troops had the task of blocking the main roads from Cannes to St. Raphael. No information is available about the operations of these troops, but presumably they were successful since no counter-attacks developed on D-day from the direction of Cannes. At 0100 the mark boats, which in this sector included two destroyers, took station and minesweeping commenced. The channels and boat lanes into Blue and Green beaches were swept but no mines were found, neither were there any underwater obstacles. The gun support ships and the convoys of combat loaders, L.S.T., L.C.I., and L.C.T. arrived on time. The bombardment was effective and all major targets were destroyed or neutralised by 0800 with the exception of one coastal battery near St. Raphael, which gave some trouble until it was later destroyed, while the fire of the rocket craft was as devastating as in Alpha and Delta areas. The arrangements and organisation of the assault waves was similar to what has already been described for "Alpha" sector.

The first waves reached the beaches with the loss of two L.C.V.P. sunk by machine-gun fire near Green beach, and at 0800 one battalion of the 141st R.C.T. landed on Blue beach while three minutes later the other two battalions of the 141st R.C.T. commenced landing on Green beach followed by the whole of the 143rd R.C.T. Immediately after the first wave of infantry, two L.C.T. landed amphibious tanks on Green beach. All troops and vehicles were landed dry-shod, and Green beach was found to be better than had been anticipated, though for a time it was under machine-gun fire, and after 0930 some artillery fire was directed against it, hitting and inflicting damage on L.S.T.*51* and L.C.T.339, *610* and *625*.[1] Unloading at Blue beach was completed by 1100. The Commanding General of the 36th Division landed with his staff at 1000 having already asked that the 142nd R.C.T. should be put ashore on Red beach at 1400.

Now occurred the only mishap of a triumphant day. At 1110 the minesweepers engaged in sweeping the approaches to Red beach were heavily shelled and obliged to retire. At 1230 an S.C. boat led eight shallow water sweepers towards the beach. The sweepers came under a heavy barrage at 1,700 yards from the beach but continued to within 500 yards of the shore when they were compelled to withdraw still under fire. From 1220 to 1330 heavy bombers attacked Red beach, at 1310 the Gunfire Support

1 The British L.C.T. 307 was hit by shellfire and abandoned on D-day, but M03316/45, the interrogation report of one of the crew, does not say in which sector this took place. This casualty is not mentioned by Admiral Hewitt except that the craft is shown as damaged in p. 53 of the report.

Group commenced a bombardment and a little later twelve drone boats were sent in. Three drones duly exploded on the beach but the others either did not explode or ran wild on the way in. Arrangements had been made for the "Camel" rocket craft to be reinforced by L.C.T.(R) from the other two sectors but some of these were delayed[1] and the approaching assault craft came under heavy fire. Under these circumstances the Beach Assault Commander reported to Rear-Admiral Lewis, who was in command in "Camel" area, that it would be advisable to postpone the assault till1430.

By this time the presence of a dense minefield in the Gulf of Fréjus had been reported, while the progress of the troops ashore had been so good that the early capture of St. Raphael and Red beach seemed probable, and in these circumstances Admiral Lewis cancelled the assault at 1415 and ordered that the 142nd R.C.T. should be landed at 1515 over Green beach where unloading was proceeding smoothly. This was done, but it had not been possible to inform the divisional headquarters of the change in plan. From 1930 to 2000 the Fréjus—St. Raphael area was bombarded from the sea preparatory to the assault from landward, and the enemy's resistance was overcome, though the two towns were not occupied till next day. Yellow beach had already been occupied by American troops; at 1915 the net across the entrance of the Rade d'Agay was removed, and an hour later Yellow beach was open for some traffic. No mines were swept in the Rade d'Agay, but the first craft to touch down at Yellow beach, L.C.I.951, set off a whole row of land mines at the water's edge, and sustained damage. Sweeping of the Gulf of Fréjus was recommenced, and Red beach was opened at 1900 on 17th August, but it required two more days of intensive effort completely to clear the small Gulf of 90 shallow-laid moored mines and 15 moored magnetic mines; during this operation five craft were mined, four of which were sunk.[2]

At 2043 a force of about four Dornier 217 approached "Camel" area at 15,000 feet dropping to 8,000 feet. Bombs were dropped near the *Bayfield,* Admiral Lewis' flagship, and one glider bomb was released which destroyed L.S.T.*282* and two L.C.V.P. which were off the beach at St. Raphael. The control plane employed a new technique operating over the land, so that it was able to keep its victim between it and our jamming ships. Although twenty-two ships were trying to jam the missile they were unable to control it.[3] This was the only bombing attack made against the naval forces on 15th August.

The bombardment forces in the "Camel" area consisted of the battleship *Arkansas,* the cruisers *Tuscaloosa, Brooklyn, Marblehead, Argonaut, Duguay Trouin* and *Emile Bertin* and eleven American destroyers. The *Arkansas* fired 383 rounds of 12-inch[4] against batteries near Anthéor and St. Raphael, the *Tuscaloosa* fired 581 rounds, the *Marblehead* 628, and the *Brooklyn* 528 at troops, batteries and defences using aircraft from the *Brooklyn* for spotting, though some shoots were controlled by shore parties and at times the ships approached sufficiently close to do their own spotting. The *Emile Bertin* was still more heavily engaged, firing 828 rounds, but the *Duguay Trouin* had little opportunity for firing. The *Argonaut* fired 394 rounds during the day, largely at batteries between Cannes and Antibes and on Ile Ste. Marguérite, coming under fairly heavy fire; later in the day she moved to the Gulf of Fréjus, where she joined in the bombardments. The destroyers bore their full share of the bombardment, usually approaching sufficiently

1 H. p. 192.
2 These craft were Y.M.S.24, P.T.218, P.T.202, M.L.563 sunk, B.Y.M.S.2022 damaged.
3 H. p. 46.
4 Bombardment figures are taken from H. diagram 20.

near the target to spot their own fall of shot. The *Ordronaux* was particularly heavily engaged. In the afternoon the *Philadelphia,* and two French destroyers arrived from "Delta" area and reinforced the "Camel" ships, some of which must have been running short of ammunition. The result of the delay in capturing Red beach was that the French armoured brigade, which had arrived had to postpone landing till next day, when it was put ashore in "Delta" sector.[1]

24. The Airborne Assault

The mission of the Provisional Troop Carrier Airborne Division was to carry the parachute troops and tow the glider-borne elements of the 1st Airborne Task Force to the drop and landing zones in the Argens Valley between Le Muy and Carnoules. The Airborne Task Force, which was commanded by Brigadier-General R. T. Frederick, consisted of the British 2nd Independent Parachute Brigade, the American 517th Parachute R.C.T. and two additional American parachute battalions together with the 550th Infantry Battalion (Glider) and supporting troops. The objective of this force was to block the movement of enemy reserves into the assault area from the north and northwest. During the planning stage Admiral Hewitt was concerned to make certain that a corridor was chosen through which the aircraft could fly without being fired on by allied ships or beach anti-aircraft guns, and as a result there was no single case reported of troop carrier aircraft being fired on by allied guns. To assist the aircraft to reach landfall at Le Trayas three beacon ships, the *Stuart Prince, Antwerp,* and P.T.209, were stationed in the centre of the corridor at thirty-mile intervals before 0300 on 15th August.

The aircraft took off from their bases near Rome in the early morning. The first Pathfinder aircraft made landfall at about 0315, followed an hour later by 396 troop carriers, which returned to their bases after dropping the paratroops. The departure of the glider-borne force had to be postponed for two hours but at 1015 the gliders, towed by 71 aircraft, were cut loose over the drop zone. Later in the day reinforcements and supplies were flown in mainly by gliders. In all, the aircraft made 807 sorties, 446 carrying paratroops and 361 towing gliders, for the loss of only three aircraft and nine gliders.[2] This is remarkable considering that more than half the sorties were made in darkness and that there was a dense fog over the drop zones. Though the fog caused a number of troops to be landed some distance from the scheduled area, a high percentage was dropped in or very close to the drop zones.[3]

The airborne troops accomplished their mission with great success, and a decisive factor in the development of the allied plan was the exploitation of the wedge driven into the enemy positions by the landing of this force. Through this wedge light armoured columns thrust northwards and the enemy forces were split into three separate groups.[4] On 16th August the airborne division, having concentrated its forces and mastered the enemy in the neighbourhood of the drop zones, occupied Draguignan[5] and Les Arcs. On 19th August the airborne forces reinforced by a regiment of Commandos from Port Cros, wheeled to the right for the advance to the east, but the enemy, who had retreated in haste

1 H. pp. 54 and 192.
2 H. p. 275.
3 H. p. 275. This no doubt refers to the American troops for less than half of the British brigade was dropped in the correct area.
4 H. p. 275.
5 Information about the advance of the airborne troops is taken from H. Part II, Chapter 1.

at other points, offered a bitter resistance in the region towards the Italian frontier and was reinforced by troops from the German armies in Italy. Not till 25th August did the Airborne force enter Cannes and Antibes, after which stiff opposition was met on the east bank of the River Var, which was crossed on the 27th; on the 28th Nice was occupied.

The German retreat from Nice was covered by demolitions and minefields slowing down our advance, and such stiff resistance did the enemy offer that in spite of considerable support from naval bombardments (*see Section* 40) the Airborne Task Force only reached the line Utele-Sospel-Monaco on 5th September. By 12th September our troops had reached Menton on the coast, and repelled a counter-attack; for some days they had to remain on the defensive near the coast, though inland they started to penetrate the mountain passes towards the Italian frontier. On 25th September, on which day Operation "Dragoon" may be considered to have terminated, our troops were holding a line roughly along the Franco-Italian frontier from St. Antonin (3½ miles North of Menton) to a point on the coast some three miles to the west of Ventimiglia.

It may be of interest to add a few details about the operations of the 2nd Parachute Brigade of three battalions, the only British troops to take part in the invasion of the south of France; the information is taken from the war diary of the Brigade. Dropping was inaccurate, for though the 6th Battalion was 70% intact, the 4th and 5th were very scattered, groups landing as far afield as Fayence and Cannes.[1] Headquarters were established at Le Mitan by 0615, and the 6th Battalion captured La Motte. Reinforcements arrived during the afternoon, and by 2000 the artillery was in fair strength while many of the scattered parties had joined up with their units. The actual landing was unopposed and though later on resistance was encountered, it was never serious, and by the close of day all objectives had been reached, all counterattacks repulsed and many prisoners taken. Le Muy was attacked during the night; this attack failed, but the town was occupied at 1500 next day. During the 17th a considerable quantity of supplies was flown in and the brigade occupied Fayence and Callas, but during the night, the force holding Les Quatre Chemins, two miles south-east of Callas, was counter-attacked and had to withdraw, retaining contact with the enemy, who retreated next morning. During the 18th the brigade was withdrawn into army reserve. On 20th August the British force moved to the front and some skirmishing took place. The brigade continued in action with the enemy but fighting was not heavy and on the 25th it occupied Cannes. Next day the British force embarked and left the area.

25. The Special Operations Group

The purpose of the operations of this group, commanded by Captain Johnson U.S.N., was to deceive the enemy about the exact point of landing of the expedition once he had realised that an invasion was imminent at some point between Genoa and the Spanish frontier. This deception was to be brought about by threatening successively the Genoa area, the Nice-Cannes area, and the Cette-Agde area, with groups of small craft which would simulate powerful invasion forces. Two groups were formed, the eastern consisting of the *Aphis, Scarab, Antwerp, Stuart Prince,* four -M.Ls, and twelve P.Ts., while the western group comprised the destroyer *Endicott,* four M.Ls., eight P.Ts. and twelve A.S.R.C.

1 The fourth Battalion was only 30–40% intact while the 5th could only raise one company.

The eastern group, less the P.Ts. sailed from Ajaccio during the morning of 14th August, with fighter cover to prevent it being sighted by the enemy's reconnaissance aircraft, and at 2130 was joined by the P.Ts. which had been based at Bastia. Three P.Ts, were detached to form an anti-E boat screen off Nice, and another four to land the French Commandos in the Gulf of La Napoule, as related in *Section* 23. The main group continued north as if heading for Genoa, simulating a large force with the aid of radar jamming and the creation of many artificial radar targets from aircraft and reflector balloons. At 2230 the *Antwerp* and *Stuart Prince* were detached to take station as beacon ships for the transport aircraft and at 2330 the remainder of the group altered course to the westward. The P.Ts. which had landed the Commandos rejoined and took station to the eastward of the group to guard the force against E-boats.

At 0420, 15th August, the group arrived off Antibes and the gunboats carried out a bombardment of targets between Antibes and the Var river while the M.Ls. and remaining P.Ts, employed radio counter-measures to distract the enemy's attention from the *Aphis* and *Scarab.* These measures were successful, for most of the enemy's fire was directed at the decoy screen and the gunboats were not hit. The bombardment was maintained for about an hour, after which the force proceeded to Briande Bay in "Alpha" sector, where it joined the Western group, releasing the P.Ts. which were sent to augment the screening forces.

The *Endicott* and M.Ls. of the western group sailed from Ajaccio on 14th August, about two hours later than the eastern group and were joined at 2100 when about 25 miles south of the Hyères islands by the P.Ts. and A.S.R.C. from Calvi. Reflector balloons were streamed and radio counter-measures commenced by the unit and by covering aircraft, to simulate a convoy twelve miles long and eight wide, a much larger force than the "Sitka" Attack Force, which was then moving up to its assault position. At 0100 15th August, the group turned towards La Ciotat and as the radar station on Cape Sicié had purposely been left unmolested, it was hoped that the enemy would track this movement. Fog and radar failures somewhat interfered with the programme, but the *Endicott* and two of the M.Ls. opened fire on shore-positions near La Ciotat at 0300. Dummy radio traffic was put on the air imitating a force flagship, vessels of an amphibious attack force, and a fighter direction ship controlling night fighters. To heighten the illusion the A.S.R.C. were to enter La Ciotat Bay and after laying a smoke screen, put down a beach barrage, and simulate a landing; in the event however, only one craft actually entered the bay.

Except for a few rounds of anti-aircraft fire, the enemy made no opposition. The force withdrew and had joined the eastern group in Briande Bay by 1100. To continue the mystification of the enemy, at 0400 aircraft dropped 300 dummy paratroops rigged with demolition charges to the north-west of Toulon. These operations seem to have caused considerable confusion to the enemy, for during the first two days of the assault German announcements credited the Allies with landings on a front stretching from Cannes to the westward of Toulon, while on D-day it was stated that Cannes had been captured and that a force of battleships had bombarded Antibes and Nice. Another German claim was that an attempted landing to the east of Marseilles had been frustrated by the assault force running into a minefield.[1] Thus it is very probable that these operations retarded the arrival of German reinforcements in the real assault area.

A second simulated landing was to have been staged at La Ciotat during the night of the 15th/16th, but owing to the failure of a tanker to arrive the force could not refuel in

1 H. p. 179.

time, and the operation was postponed for twenty-four hours; even then some of the P.Ts. were not ready and had to be left behind. The second diversionary operation commenced at 1600 on 15th August, when the *Aphis, Scarab,* and four M.Ls. sailed from Briande Bay, followed four hours later by the *Endicott* with four P.Ts. and thirteen A.S.R.C., who overtook the gunboats at 2300. After arriving off La Ciotat a bombardment was carried out between 0310 and 0435, while four waves of A.S.R.C., simulating an assault, entered the bay, fired rockets and made smoke. The enemy was thoroughly alarmed and opened a heavy fire against the imaginary gunfire support and transport areas, but the smoke screens and rapid manoeuvres enabled the craft to evade the barrage and no serious hits were sustained. The Germans claimed to have repulsed the assault of a strong force whose convoy was twelve miles long, which was the exact convoy size which the radar counter-measure plan intended to convey.[1]

During the retirement one of the A.S.R.C. picked up two radar targets, which were thought to be friendly vessels until they opened fire. The A.S.R.C. employed evasive tactics until 0555 when the two gunboats arrived. The *Aphis* and *Scarab* continued the action and were joined by the *Endicott* at 0609, but the enemy, which turned out to be the escort ships *Caprioio* and *Konid Allah* continued fighting until 0730, when they were sunk thirteen miles off La Croisette point, the southern point of Marseilles Ray, 211 prisoners being taken. The *Endicott* was hit by one small calibre shell and by splinters and had three men wounded while one of the A..S.R.C. sustained slight damage. The diversion unit returned to the assault area, and on 18th August, the Special Operations Group was dissolved, the British gunboats being released to the C.-in-C. Mediterranean while the remainder of the craft were assigned other tasks in the assault area.

26. Naval Off-Shore Movements in Assault Area, 15th–17th August

As soon as the transports, combat loaders and L.S.I. had unloaded, they were formed into convoys and sailed from the area. So rapid was the unloading that seven ships due to sail on 16th August, and two on 17th, were able to depart on D-day; in all 95 vessels organised into four convoys were sailed from the area before the close of 15th August.[2] Control of convoys and of escorts was exercised by C.T.G. 80.6, Captain Clay U.S.N., in U.S.S. *Jouett,* assisted by two other destroyers and some P.Ts. stationed in Briande Bay. A convoy assembly area was set up ten miles east of Cape Camarat for merchant vessels bound for Naples and Ajaccio and for all L.S.T., while all other landing craft and merchant vessels bound for Oran assembled ten miles east-south-east of Cape Camarat. Two convoys arrived in the area on D-day after the assault, one of these being Special Convoy No. 2 from Oran, containing the French Armoured Brigade, which was to have landed at once over "Camel" Red beach.

As explained in *Section* 23 disembarkation was delayed, and landing commenced at noon on the 16th over the "Delta" beaches. The second convoy was S.M.2 from Naples consisting of store ships. On 16th August the convoy control handled 76 ingoing and 86 outgoing ships, including among the former convoy T.F.1 from Taranto, containing

1 H. p. 179.
2 H. p. 52.

two French infantry divisions of the 2nd Corps, which commenced landing at 1800 over "Alpha" beaches. On 17th August, one convoy arrived and five departed. Thereafter convoy movements were regularly carried out and in general arrangements worked smoothly; though some mistakes did occur owing to lack of information, the planned schedule was met and in some cases accelerated.[1] General Patch, commanding the Seventh Army, landed with his staff on the 16th, and set up his headquarters at St. Tropez, taking over the command of the troops which in accordance with American practice had up till then been exercised by Admiral Hewitt.

The bombardments on D-day have already been fully considered in *Sections* 19-23. During the day 15,900 rounds of 5-inch and above were fired.[2] During the night of 15th-16th the Gun Support Groups withdrew from the area, returning at dawn. On the 16th Admiral Rodgers released the "Delta" bombardment ships, no further gun support being required in that sector, though during that day the *Fitch* and *Hobson* of his force, carried out some shoots against targets which were just inside the "Camel" area. In "Alpha" area there were during the 16th some bombardments of points between Cape Nègre and Le Lavandou and "Alpha" gun support ships also co-operated with the "Sitka" force for the reduction of Port Cros. In "Camel" area, bombardments continued on the 16th, the *Argonaut* and *Ellyson* being heavily engaged against troops and vehicles inland of the line St. Raphael-Agay, and the *Brooklyn* also carried out some shoots. Other ships of the force bombarded positions on the extreme right flank of the army and targets near Cannes and Antibes.

On the 17th the "Alpha" and "Camel" gun support ships were released and Admiral Davidson henceforth exercised control over all bombardment forces. He organised his command so that two battleships, two heavy and six light cruisers, and eleven destroyers remained in the assault area, while the others withdrew into reserve at Algiers, Palermo, or Naples, being sent into the assault area to relieve as required. On 17th August, Admiral Hewitt released the *Jeanne D' Arc,* and *Sirius*[3] which had been held in reserve at Naples. The American cruiser *Omaha* arrived in the assault area on the 16th.

As soon as the assault commenced, the screening plan was put into operation. The in-shore screens controlled by the Task Force Commanders and consisting, of P.Cs., S.Cs., L.Cs., L.C.C., L.C.V.P. and L.C.M.(S), were established principally to provide smoke protection; the larger craft in addition acted as a screen against U-boats, E-boats and limpeteers and were reinforced by minesweepers at dawn and dusk. The two outer screens were controlled by C.T.G. 80.6 in the *Jouett;*[4] of these two, the inner, consisting of five destroyers, was concerned with defence against E-boats and U-boats, and also provided anti-aircraft defence of the convoy assembly areas, while the main destroyer screen consisted of all ships not required for other duties and provided cover for the entire assault area except the south-west section of "Alpha" sector where destroyers could not operate owing to minefields in Hyères Roads; this gap was filled at night by a patrol of P.Ts. The original screen, 50 miles in length, was composed of 26 destroyers, but the number naturally varied from time to time. So far as is known no attempt was made by enemy forces to penetrate the screen during the first three days of the operation. The C.-in-C Mediterranean in his

1 H. p. 227.
2 H. p. 52.
3 The Sirius, however, took part in the later stages of the operation, see Section 37.
4 This officer, Captain Clay, U.S.N., in addition to controlling the screen and being in command of all escorts, was responsible for the reception and despatch of all convoys.

despatch[1] gives the opinion that an "endless chain" patrol, which is the normal British practice, would have been more efficient from the anti-submarine point of view, than this arrangement whereby a number of ships carried out independant patrols. By 18th August, all minesweeping in the assault area having been completed, the sweepers were removed from the command of the Task Force Commanders, and came under the orders of C.T.G. 80.10, Commander Messmer U.S.N., in the Barricade. The heavy programme of sweeping which was then carried out will be considered in the next chapter.

27. The Beaches. Enemy Opposition

Unloading over the beaches was carried out in a very satisfactory manner, the lessons of earlier landing operations having been well learned, and but few complaints were made about congestion on the beaches, which was so prevalent during the Salerno landing. Three naval beach battalions were assigned, one to each sector and a naval liaison officer, appointed to co-ordinate the activities of all three, established his headquarters with the Commander of the Army Beach Control Group near Ste. Maxime. The beaches were well adapted for landing craft though less satisfactory from the Army point of view as the exits often left much to be desired. Twenty-four pontoon causeways with crews were available, twelve for "Alpha", four for "Delta" and eight for "Camel", but they were subsequently redistributed according to the requirements of the sectors. In some places L.S.T. and in most places L.C.T. were able to discharge directly over the beaches so that there was a surplus of pontoons, but this was soon absorbed as ports were captured, for the pontoons were then used there as piers, ramps, and barges.

All L.C.T. were retained in the assault area for unloading purposes; these and the army DUKWS were augmented by 218 L.C.M., 170 of which were loaded on merchant ships and the remainder on the two L.S.G. and one L.S.C., though most of the latter (48 craft) were released and left the area with their parent ships on 18th August. The L.C.M. were mainly used for unloading vehicles, and were found to be better than L.C.T. for this purpose. The crews of these craft, of the L.C.T., and the repair personnel, established an enviable record in maintaining the craft in service under arduous conditions over a long period.[2] The main difficulty encountered on the beaches was shortage of labour and of vehicles to transfer stores from the beaches to the dumps,[3] while crews of merchant ships were not always as co-operative as might have been expected. A shortage of cargo nets in the store ships was another factor of delay, while dunnage thrown overboard by ships at anchor off the shore and wire rope and lines discarded by L.S.T. as they approached the beaches constituted obstacles to the landing craft.[4] So far as shortage of vehicles and of labour was concerned, the fault lay with the Army, in fact the facilities provided by the Navy for delivery of cargo to the beaches far exceeded the capacity of the Army to unload and transfer it from the beaches to supply dumps; on this account one of the Task Force Commanders recommended that the Navy should take over the responsibility of handling all stores as far as the supply dumps. Admiral Hewitt however disagreed with this.[5]

1 M05662/45. C.-in-C. Med. report p. 3.
2 H. p. 337.
3 H. p. 337.
4 H. p. 337.
5 H. p. 338.

In spite of these difficulties 86,575 men and 12,520 vehicles were landed during the first three days, besides over 46,000 tons of stores. On 16th August, the French armoured brigade and the two divisions of the French 2nd Corps commenced landing, the former over "Delta" beaches and the latter over "Alpha". On this day both Fréjus and St. Raphael were captured and work commenced on preparing the latter port to receive ships and craft. In "Delta" sector Blue beach was closed, but the port of St. Tropez was opened to traffic. In "Alpha" sector Red beach was cleared of mines and reopened and exits were constructed, while on 17th August, "Camel" Red beach was opened. On 17th August, the C.-in-C. Mediterranean closed his advance headquarters at Ajaccio and returned to Naples.

Enemy opposition was surprisingly light. The small amount of gunfire has been commented on in the sections dealing with the assault on each sector, and the solitary air raid on 15th August, has been described in *Section* 23. On 16th August at 2050 five Junkers 88 escorted by four fighters approached St. Tropez and dropped anti-personnel bombs on the "Delta" beaches, the resulting casualties being 14 killed and 36 wounded. On the same day at dusk the American destroyer *C. F. Hughes,* stationed in the eastern sector of the screen, reported that a glider bomb fell near her. Next day two enemy fighters approached "Alpha" area at 1900 but were driven off, one being destroyed, and at 2138 a Junkers 88 came in low and fast but was shot down by U.S.S. *Champlin.* At 2040 occurred the biggest raid so far, when six Junkers 88 dropped bombs near St. Raphael and Ste. Maxime without doing any damage. The allied naval losses during the first three days were:- sunk; 1 L.S.T. and 2 L.C.V.P. by glider bomb, 2 L.C.V.P. by gunfire, 2 P.T., 1 Y.M.S. and 1 M.L. by mines; damaged: 6 L.C.T. by gunfire, 3 L.C.T., 8 L.C.I., 1 L.C.C., 5 L.C.V.P., 1 M.L. and 1 B.Y.M.S. by mines or under-water obstacles, 1 S.C. by a run-away drone, and H.M.S. *Brave* and 1 L.C.T. in collision. No day to day figures are given for naval personnel casualties but they were extremely small.

With the close of 17th August, the first phase of operation "Dragoon" came to an end.

28. The Carrier Force

The Carrier Force (T.F.88) was commanded by Rear-Admiral Troubridge, flying his flag in the *Royalist.* The force was divided into two groups, T.G.88.1, under the direct command of Admiral Troubridge, consisting of the *Royalist Delhi, Attacker, Emperor, Khedive, Searcher* and *Pursuer* escorted by the *Troubridge* (D.24), five British destroyers and one Greek destroyer. Rear-Admiral Durgin, U.S.N., in the *Tulagi,* commanded T.G.88.2 which comprised the *Caledon, Colombo, Stalker, Hunter* and the two American carriers *Tulagi* and *Kasaan Bay,* escorted by six American destroyers. The British carriers had embarked squadrons numbers 807, 809, 879 and 899 ("Seafires") 881 and 898 ("Wildcats") and 800 ("Hellcats"), while each of the American ships carried a squadron of "Hellcats"; each carrier accommodated about 24 aircraft. In addition twelve night fighters were based at Casabianda and Solenzara in Corsica, to be flown on to the carriers if necessary. The task of the Carrier Force was to provide the greatest possible fighter protection over the beaches, to supply spotting aircraft for the bombardment groups, to send close support missions and to provide for its own protection against enemy aircraft and U-boats. Owing to the weakness of the enemy's resistance, the functions of protection and spotting tended to become less important and the emphasis was aid on strafing and bombing.

The Carrier Force arrived off the assault area in the early morning of 15th August, and the first aircraft took off at 0610. The patrols first carried out their bombing or strafing missions and then patrolled over the beaches. Once they had left the carriers the aircraft came under the orders of the Air Task Force Commander, Brigadier-General G. P. Saville. The carriers operated during the day in an area about thirty miles south of the beaches. The two groups of ships worked independently but generally kept within visual signalling distance of each other. The wind was light all day, but deck landings were made without difficulty. Conditions ashore were not very favourable, especially early in the day, for low clouds made accurate bombing difficult. Altogether 170 sorties were flown on D-day from T.G.88.1.[1]

The system of control was that on each flight taking off, the Fighter Direction Officer of the Carrier Force notified the air control ship in the assault area of the type of aircraft and other particulars, also the targets on which the aircraft had been briefed. When the patrol reached the assault area its leader called in to the *Ulster Queen,* if on a patrol mission, or to the *Catoctin,* if on an offensive mission, for confirmation of targets or assignment of a new mission. While in the forward area, the flight remained under the control of the forward control ship, to which the aircraft reported their departure from the area on the completion of the mission. The control ship then informed the flagship of the Carrier Force of the release of the mission and the fact that it was on its return journey.[2] Later in the operation when the Air Commander had left the flagship and had established headquarters ashore, the *Royalist* assumed control of the offensive missions.

Our aircraft encountered no enemy fighters and in general the enemy's anti-aircraft fire was not heavy, so casualties were small. Two of the *Pursuer's* aircraft were obliged to land in the sea owing to shortage of fuel, the pilots not having been able to locate the Carrier Force. The pilots were picked up by a Catalina at 1250 and were taken to Ajaccio where they obtained transport to Casabianda airfield. Next day they flew off to the ship in two spare aircraft arriving back at 1700.[3] The last aircraft landed on at 2035 upon which the Carrier Force retired southward.

During the day each group of carriers had kept in compact formation near a previously decided "datum point" with the destroyers disposed so as to give a maximum of anti-submarine protection while permitting them readily to assume close anti-aircraft stations if necessary. Normally the carriers turned into the wind together for flying off or landing on, except when only one or two aircraft were involved; on these occasions the carrier concerned would leave the formation escorted by one destroyer and manoeuvre as necessary to recover or launch the aircraft. The two American carriers had a two knot advantage in speed over the British and Admiral Durgin at times found that this factor made it difficult to keep his formation closed up at high speeds.[4] The carriers sustained no attack from the enemy, but during the night flares were dropped near the force without subsequent developments. The three flight deck L.S.T., which were equipped with G.C.I., had arrived in the assault area as scheduled and they launched their aircraft at 0930, assisting during the day as fighter control ships, while after dark they controlled the night fighters. The Fighter Defence Tender was in charge of anti-aircraft defence and air raid

1 The sorties were made up as follows : Spotting 32, Reconnaissance 6, Fighter Bomber 76, Beach Cover 32, Force Cover 24. Seafires made 66 sorties, Hellcats 42 and Wildcats 62. (M057950/44 App. B.) No figures are available for T.G.88.2

2 H. p. 270.

3 M010202/44 R. of P. Pursuer p. 3.

4 H. p. 194.

warnings; owing to the passivity of the Luftwaffe the tender found little employment of this nature, but she also controlled the defensive fighter patrols.

The Carrier Force was back in position by daybreak (16th August) and the first aircraft was flown off at 0610. Sorties were made regularly according to schedule and the force again withdrew during the night. As the operation progressed, it became evident that little air defence of the beaches was required and this function was taken over by shore based aircraft when landing strips had been laid out on 19th August; at the same time there was less call for spotting aircraft, and so fighter bomber and armed reconnaissance missions became the most important duties of the carrier borne aircraft. On 17th August, aircraft from the *Emperor* and *Khedive* took part in the attack on the fort at Port Cros, which was partly protected from the ships' gunfire by the lie of the land, and had been resisting for three days. The aircraft dropped 500 lb. bombs on the fort which soon after surrendered. The "datum point" for the carriers' operations was changed each day, and on 18th August, the operating area of the carriers was moved to the westward and further inshore. By this time the missions flown were mainly up the Rhône valley and owing to the short range of the Seafires, it was necessary for the carriers to approach the coast as much as possible. Had the enemy's air force been active, this would have been a dangerous move, but as it was, the only danger apprehended was from minefields, which obliged the force to remain outside the hundred fathom line. On 19th August, a flight from the *Emperor* was returning from an attack on a railway yard when, while crossing the Rhône estuary, two E-boats were sighted and attacked; one was destroyed but the other though repeatedly hit, managed to escape.[1] The same day an aircraft from the *Pursuer* piloted by Sub-Lieutenant R. Banks, R.N.V.R., was shot down between Orange and Avignon. The Pilot succeeded in ditching his aircraft in the Rhône; evading the Germans he joined up with the "maquis" and finally after many adventures returned to his ship at Maddalena on 28th August.[2]

29.

On 19th August, Admiral Troubridge with T.G.88.1 retired to Maddalena to refuel the ships and rest the crews, leaving Admiral Durgin in command, and returned to the assault area on the 21st, when T.G.88.2 retired to Maddalena for a spell, arriving back on the 24th. On 20th August, one of the *Hunter's* aircraft, whose pilot had been badly wounded and was probably unconscious, crashed on landing and brought down the H.F./D.F. mast, causing the death of six ratings and of the pilot himself.[3]

Strikes were carried out against the retreating German columns with much effect, the *Emperor's* aircraft making a particularly successful series of attacks on 21st August, by which time the carriers were operating at a point 25 miles south of Marseilles. During the ensuing days aircraft penetrated as far as 120 miles up the Rhône valley, causing havoc to the long columns of retreating enemy vehicles. General Saville in a message to Admiral Troubridge said that he had personally counted 202 destroyed enemy vehicles near Le Luc and St. Maximin.[4] On 24th August, T.G.88.1 retired to Maddalena followed by the *Stalker* and *Hunter* from T.G.88.2 on the 26th. On 27th August, the British carriers were

1 M010202/44 R. of P. Emperor. p. 4
2 M010202/44 R. of P. Pursuey App. J..
3 M04533/45 R. of P. Hunter p. 5.
4 H. p. 270.

released from the operation by Admiral Hewitt, and the force sailed for Alexandria. The American carriers left the assault area on 29th August, on which day Task Force 88 was dissolved. The Air Sea Rescue Service functioned admirably and between 10th August and 29th August rescued 80 air crews from the sea, the majority of these being from land-based aircraft.[1] Altogether 1627 sorties were flown from the British carriers[2] but no figures are available for the American ships.

Aircraft casualties in the seven British carriers were 13 lost on enemy territory and 12 forced landings, all but one in the sea. In addition there were 40 deck landing accidents though in many of these cases the aircraft were repaired. The reports contain no figures for American casualties. No aircraft was damaged in aerial combat; in fact there was only one encounter with the enemy in the air when some of our aircraft came across three Junkers 52; on this incident Admiral Troubridge makes the terse comment: "Easy meat". Admiral Troubridge does not mention the date, but according to Admiral Hewitt, (H. p. 64) on 19th August, aircraft from T.G.88.2 destroyed five enemy bombers and damaged one; neither the *Hunter* nor the *Stalker,* however, mention this incident.

Owing to the enemy's quiescence, there was little employment for the anti-aircraft cruisers. In his reports Admiral Troubridge commented on the fact that the detailed air plan was completed without the Rear-Admiral Escort Carriers (then Rear-Admiral Bissett) being represented, and that the plan arrived too late for adequate study. Admiral Troubridge remarked that in the plan too little allowance was made for the limitations of carriers and of naval aircraft. As the final details of the plan were only received the day before sailing the Admiral thought it better to try to surmount the difficulties rather than request last minute alterations.[3] Admiral Troubridge considered that the squadrons were not sufficiently well trained for the variety of duties they had to perform and that the small number of casualties incurred was a reflection of the inadequacy of the enemy rather than of the skill of our pilots.[4]

Admiral Troubridge was of the opinion that six carriers was the maximum number which could be handled tactically by one flagship but that four would be the best number. With the facilities available in the *Royalist,* however, five carriers was the maximum with which the air direction team could have coped.[5] He further considered that the destroyer screen would have been too weak had the enemy submarines been at all active.[6] Admiral Troubridge ascribed the increase of deck landing accidents in the later days of the operation to fatigue on the part of the pilots.[7]

In his final report[8] Admiral Troubridge again laid stress on the fatigue not only of the pilots but also of the communication and deck landing personnel, and insisted on an improved standard of training for pilots. He asserted that the Hellcat was the ideal type of carrier borne aircraft for assault operations,[9] while paying tribute to the many good qualities of the Seafire, and emphasised that the rocket projectile, with which only the American Hellcats were equipped, was a far better weapon than the bomb for strafing,

1 M02673/45 p. 15.
2 T.F.88.1 (5 ships) had 983 sorties, the Hunter 307 and the Stalker 337.
3 M057950/44 Rear-Admiral Troubridge's Preliminary Report p. 2.
4 M057950/44 p. 4.
5 M057950/44 p. 4.
6 M057950/44 p. 5.
7 M057950/44 p. 5.
8 M010202/44.
9 M010204/44 p. 15.

but that bombs were more effective against enclosed batteries.[1] Admiral Troubridge was also strongly of the opinion that a cruiser of the *Royalist* type was most unsuitable as the flagship of a carrier force,[2] and that for future operations of this nature the Admiral should fly his flag in a light fleet carrier. The C.-in-C. Mediterranean while agreeing with this comment,[3] expressed a doubt as to whether a fleet carrier could be made available as flagship. The C.-in-C. did not agree with the desirability of a carrier force remaining all day so close to a "datum point", in view of possible submarine attacks, and he considered that the "datum point" should have been varied from time to time each day.[4]

30. Shore-Based Air Support[5]

Fighter cover for the assault area was provided during daylight by aircraft of the 12th Tactical Air Command from bases in Corsica, and as airfields became available in Southern France either by capture or construction, fighter squadrons were also based there. Four patrols were established providing low, medium and high cover with the total number of aircraft on patrol varying from 28 to 32. Most of the low patrols and many of the medium ones were ordered on fighter bomber missions before commencing their defensive patrols. Control of fighter cover was maintained by F.D.T.13 with the *Ulster Queen* as standby, and the *Catoctin* as second standby. All patrols reported to F.D.T.13 when entering the assault area and missions were assigned. Owing to the absence of enemy activity fighters were often able to remain in the area beyond their scheduled time, and they were thus available to search for aircraft which had crashed or been forced down. When fuel permitted they circled such aircraft until the arrival of an Air Sea Rescue unit.

As the Army advanced, patrol lines were moved inland. Fighter cover for convoys up to a point forty miles from the beaches was provided by aircraft based on Corsica and Sardinia, and on August 16th a continuous patrol of twelve aircraft was maintained over the convoy lane, but the scale of effort was soon reduced when it was seen that the enemy was remaining passive. Night fighters from Corsican bases consisted of patrols of six aircraft at dusk and dawn, and of four aircraft during the remainder of the night. These patrols were controlled in the first place by F.D.T.13 or one of the G.C.I. equipped L.S.T., but later, installations were set up ashore to control the night patrols.

Bombing did not cease with the assault and up to 1430 on 15th August, the maximum fighter bomber effort was directed against such enemy batteries as had not already been silenced or overrun, and also any light batteries or other military installations capable of delaying the advance of our troops. After 1430 on D-day and on the succeeding days fighter bombers, and at times heavy bombers, were used on armed reconnaissance missions against hostile troop and vehicle concentrations, railway yards and bridges over the Rhône and Durance rivers. On D-day fighter bombers carried out about 750 sorties, most of which were successful. The first heavy bomber attack after the landing was against "Camel" Red beach where, from 1207 to 1217, bombers, 96 in number, dropped 187 tons of bombs as a preliminary to the naval assault. As already related in *Section,* 23, the assault was eventually cancelled. After the beach had been captured from the landward,

1 M010204/44 p. 18.
2 M057950/44 App.' C.
3 M011712144.
4 M011712/44.
5 The source for this section is H. pp. 257-261 and 264-266.

inspection indicated that the bombs had caused little damage to the enemy defences and that many of them had fallen into the sea.

Heavy bombing attacks were made on road bridges in the Rhône valley for the purpose of impeding the movement of enemy reserves into the assault area; 142 heavies dropped 363 tons on three bridges west of the river and on one bridge east of the river near Valence. This attack caused great disruption of traffic on the main north-south road. A group of bridges along the lower Rhône was attacked by 104 aircraft with success. The development and rapid extension of the beach head necessitated a modification of the original plan of attack against scheduled targets, as the rapid advance of the ground forces soon caused the Bomb Safety Line to pass beyond the area in which many of the planned targets lay. For this reason after 16th August, the bulk of the fighter bomber effort was directed against targets of opportunity in the enemy's rear, such as motor transport, railways, barges, bridges and troop concentrations. At times it was necessary to re-brief fighter bombers during the flight from Corsica to the assault area, in order to prevent attacks on positions which had already been taken by our forces and to assign new targets.

The reduction of the coastal batteries defending Toulon and Marseilles was the principal target for the Air Force once it was seen that the enemy was unable to offer much resistance to the army. Attacks on the forts started on 16th August and continued till 20th August, during which period 328 medium bomber sorties were flown against the forts dropping more than 600 tons of bombs, one quarter of which were of a special armour piercing type. The area was well covered and reports showed that a good concentration on the targets was obtained with several direct hits. Damage was also done to warships in Toulon, the cruiser *La Gallissonnière* being sunk and the *Strasbourg* damaged during a raid on 17th August. Bombing of the Marseilles defences was continued until 27th August, 85 tons of bombs being dropped on the 25th, over 70 tons on the 26th and 146 tons on the 27th.[1] A heavy raid on Genoa was carried out on 4th September. No details of this raid are given in Admiral Hewitt's report, and it may be that the bombers used did not form part of the Air Commander's forces. The raid at all events was very successful and resulted in the destruction of the destroyer *Squadrista,* one torpedo boat, five submarines and three escort vessels.[2]

31. Progress of Seventh Army[3]

It has already been said that little resistance was offered by the enemy to the landing and advance of our troops, though there was a certain amount of mortar and small arms fire. Contact was made with elements of the German 242nd Infantry Division. The only counter-attack put up by the enemy was against the French Commandos near Cape Nègre and this was repulsed. All three American infantry divisions advanced rapidly, and leading elements of the 3rd Division were soon in Grimaud, while the 45th reached Plan de la Tour, and the 36th fanning out rapidly, attained the high ground overlooking Théoule, and the ridge overlooking Fréjus. During D-day 2,041 prisoners were taken, mostly troops of low category, many being Poles. During 16th August, the enemy's resistance stiffened somewhat, and a counter attack on our right flank was delivered but repulsed.

1 H. Diagram 22.

2 H. p. 97.

3 The main source for this section is H., Part 2, Chapter 1. (The action of the airborne division has already been described in Section 24).

In the north, however, the German efforts at opposition were scattered and uncoordinated. The 3rd Division occupied Collobrières and Carnoules; one force reached Flassans sur Issole while another arrived near La Londe les Maures. The 45th Division moved through Vidaubon and reached Taradeau while the 36th, having consolidated its position near Théoule moved to near Vidaubon and Camp de Cais. The first regiment of Commandos remained on Port Cros Island, but the 2nd and 3rd were transported to the mainland and they assembled near Sylvabelle. The French armoured brigade started landing over "Delta" beaches at noon and moved to its assembly area near Gonfaron and the Second French Corps started to disembark over "Alpha" beaches during the afternoon. By the close of 16th August, the "Blue Line" (*see Plan* 1) which had been laid down as the first objective, had everywhere been reached and in many places the army had advanced beyond it.[1] During the 17th enemy resistance was in general inconsiderable but elements of a new enemy division, the 148th Reserve, appeared opposite the 36th Division. This did not prevent the Americans from pushing on to Draguignan, where they captured the headquarters of the German 42nd Corps, while the 45th Division moved west to Salernes and Carces and the 3rd to the vicinity of Brignoles and Sollies-Pont. Task Force Butler, a composite force of infantry, artillery, motorised cavalry and armour, had been formed for a quick thrust to the north and during the day it arrived near Digne. It should be borne in mind that there was no front line in the normal sense of the expression but the four divisions kept in touch with each other; pockets of the enemy were sometimes left behind for future mopping up. On 18th August, elements of three new enemy divisions, the 198th, 244th and 338th were identified on the western part of the front and the 11th Panzer division was reported to be south-west of Avignon. During the day the 36th Division reached Grasse, La Bastide and Chardon; the 45th by-passed Barjols and continued to advance to the west; the 3rd Division encountered stiff resistance at Brignoles, but they captured the town and reached Roquebrussanne.

On the 19th the advance to the east was bitterly opposed but elsewhere resistance was negligible and during the day the Americans crossed the Durance near Pertuis, advanced forces reaching Sisteron. Meanwhile the disembarkation of the French 2nd Corps, of which the two remaining divisions, the 9th Colonial Infantry and the 1st Armoured, had arrived, had steadily continued and the troops advancing to the west under cover of the American 3rd Division had arrived before Toulon, the attack on which now commenced. The operations against Toulon and Marseilles will be considered in the next chapter. During 20th August, the Americans captured Aix-en-Provence against considerable opposition, and had thus out-flanked Marseilles, which was being approached by the French Corps; they also took Gap. The French by now had encircled Toulon; they had captured Banda and le Beausset, west of Toulon, and were near Hyéeres. The German forces were in full retreat up the Rhône, the 11th Panzer division acting as rearguard, and were heavily attacked by our air forces.

The 6th Corps was by now far out of reach of any naval support except on the extreme right flank, but for the sake of completeness the subsequent movements of the Seventh Army may briefly be stated. On 22nd August, troops of the 6th Corps reached the Grenoble area; on the 24th they were on the Swiss frontier near Evian, and on the same day Arles was occupied; two days later the French were in Avignon while American

1 H. p. 20.

troops occupied Carpentras and Briançon. The 28th saw the final surrender of Toulon and Marseilles, and on the last day of the month the allies reached Valence. On 3rd September, the French 1st Armoured Division entered Lyons, on the 6th the French entered Châlon-sur-Saône while the Americans were at Lons le Saunier; on 11th September, the French took Dijon and on the 12th the Americans reached Vesoul, near the Vosges.

On 15th September, General Patch's army was released by General Maitland Wilson to come under the command of General Eisenhower, taking its place on the extreme right of the Allied forces in northern France. Between 15th August and 2nd September the Seventh Anny had captured 61,716 prisoners. The Seventh Army continued to draw its supplies through ports in the South of France and long after Operation "Dragoon" was completed the allied navies gave gun support to the extreme right flank of the army, which remained near Ventimiglia.

III

THE FOLLOW UP

32. Minesweeping

Immediately after the landing the enemy commenced an extensive programme of minelaying to the westward of the assault area. The entrance to the Gulf of Fos was mined and so was the St. Louis canal, which connects the town of St. Louis and the River Rhône with the Gulf of Fos. Marseilles harbour was heavily mined as were the harbours of the coast towns, such as La Ciotat, Cannes, Nice, Bandol. An ambitious plan to mine the harbour of Toulon was put into action but was fortunately interrupted in the early stages. On 18th August, the minespotting aircraft made its first sortie, locating the minefield across the eastern entrance of Hyères Roads, and on this day Commander Messmer U.S.N., took command of all the minesweepers, which had now been released by the Assault Force Commanders. This commenced the post-assault phase, that is, the task of clearing the way into Marseilles and Toulon, though routine sweeping still had to be carried out in the anchorages off the beaches and in the approach channels. It had been expected that the enemy would endeavour to retard convoy movements by dropping mines from aircraft, but no such attempts were made and this considerably eased the strain on the minesweeping force.

On 18th August, the Bormes Roads were cleared by the 13th M/S Flotilla, and at the entrance to the Hyères Roads eleven mines were swept up; the 5th M/S Flotilla took part in the latter operation and came under fire from an enemy battery which was eventually silenced by the *Quincy;* but this interference from the enemy caused delay and sweeping was further retarded by damage to sweep gear from obstructions, while there appears to have been some doubt as to the precise area which was to be swept.[1] On 19th August, the 5th M/S Flotilla continued sweeping in Hyères Roads, and again came under fire from a battery on Esterel Point, whose fire was returned by the sweepers, and from the island of Porquerolles; during this action M.L.562 was hit aft by a 5-inch shell and had to retire, fortunately without casualties or serious damage. Again loss of sweep gear prevented much progress from being made.

Sweeping continued on the 20th and 21st after-which the 5th M/S Flotilla was relieved by the 19th M/S Flotilla and retired to Maddalena, relieving the American 21st M/S Division which had been engaged on maintenance in the Straits of Bonifacio. The clearance of Hyères Roads was eventually abandoned owing to the numerous underwater obstructions, but a channel was finally swept between Cape Benat and Esterel Point permitting access to gunfire support ships. These delays might have hindered the advance of the Army by depriving it of naval gun support on the left flank, but owing to the limited enemy resistance and the support of the guns of the 1st French Armoured Division, the lack of naval support was not much felt.[2]

1 M09992/45 R. of P. 5th M/S Flotilla p. 3.
2 H. p. 219.

Meanwhile it had been decided to enter the Gulf of Fos and occupy Port de Bouc, to provide a new point of disembarkation in the event of delay in the opening of Toulon and Marseilles, and on 24th August, the 13th M/S Flotilla commenced clearing a passage through the Gulf. The sweepers were heavily shelled by batteries situated between Cape Mèjean and Cape Couronne; for a time the sweepers persisted in their task helped by a smoke screen, but eventually sweeping had to be suspended for the day while the *Quincy, Philadelphia* and some destroyers silenced the batteries. Next day sweeping recommenced, the exact position of the mines having been ascertained by aerial reconnaissance, and the task was completed by 31st August, 173 mines, both French and German, having been accounted for. During this operation P.T.555, an L.C.M. and a French launch were mined. Although clearance was not completed until the end of August, by the 26th the shallow draught sweepers opened up the approach to Port de Bouc in spite of the enemy's fire, and a party was landed.

No detailed information is available about minesweeping operations at Toulon and Marseilles, but by 31st August, Toulon Bay and approach channel were declared safe after 74 mines had been swept, and on the same day the Marseilles entrance channel and anchorage were swept, but the complete clearance of these harbours was a lengthy operation. Toulon harbour was declared entirely safe on 12th September, after 40 shallow water contact mines had been swept, largely by the L.C.V.P. sweepers, the only casualty being Y.M.S. *21,* but the Clearance of Marseilles was still proceeding on 25th September when Operation "Dragoon" came to an end. On 4th September, the coastal channel to Nice was declared safe, and on 10th September, the port of Nice was opened; on this day the American sweeper *Seer* was mined in Hyères Roads. At Marseilles two ships were mined, the British coaster *Morialta* and the Swiss *Generoso.* On 24th September, the minesweeping force (T.G.80.10) was dissolved, and a new force was formed to complete the sweeping in coordination with the French. During the forty days following the assault the entire south coast of France had either been swept free of mines or the minefields had been located and dangerous areas declared. Six ports had been cleared.[1] In all 550 mines were swept, 463 being of the moored contact type, 70 magnetic and 17 controlled. Fortunately the Germans had used none of the new "oyster" mines in this theatre. Thirteen hitherto unknown minefields were located from the air during the 24 mine-spotting missions flown, and it is estimated that more than a thousand mines were in this way successfully by-passed.[2] No major loss was sustained from the enemy's mining effort.

33. Naval Activities off the beaches. 18th-28th August

In spite of difficulties caused by the shortage of personnel for unloading, and of vehicles, the landing of stores and equipment continued at a satisfactory rate, and the convoys arrived and departed regularly. The shortage of stevedores was to some extent eased by hiring labour on shore. Landing of the 2nd French Corps continued and the 1st French Armoured Division soon got into action with the enemy, attacking batteries which were delaying the advance of the army on Toulon.

At sea, in the assault area, sporadic attacks were made by the enemy but they accomplished little. In the early hours of 18th August, for example, four E-boats from

1 H. p. 213.
2 H. p. 213.

Monaco tried to pierce the centre of the destroyer screen but were brought to action and sunk; the *Frankford* suffered some casualties from two torpedoes, which exploded near her. At dusk on the same day five Junkers 88 attacked the "Camel" Red beach and Admiral Hewitt's flagship, the *Catoctin,* was hit by two bombs, which caused casualties amounting to 6 killed and 42 wounded. Another aircraft fired a torpedo at F.D.T.13 in the "Delta" area, but fortunately the torpedo exploded 250 yards short of the mark; the destroyer *Plunkett* shot down one of the enemy aircraft.

During the 18th, operations were commenced against the island of Porquerolles and the Gieris Peninsula, the batteries on which were hindering the minesweepers. The *Lorraine,* which had just returned to the assault area, fired 37 rounds at two batteries on the island while the *Gloire* and *Emile Bertin* fired 174 and 139 rounds respectively at batteries on the Giens Peninsula, supported by the *Quincy* (73 rounds) and the *Augusta* (39 rounds).[1] A boat was sent into Porquerolles under the white flag to demand surrender, but was fired on by the Giens batteries and forced to retire. On the same day two new beaches in the "Delta" area were opened, while on the 19th, the Gulf of Fréjus having been cleared of mines, "Camel" Red beach was put into full operation and "Camel" Yellow was closed down.

During the evening of the 19th a solitary enemy aircraft dropped a few bombs in "Camel" sector near the inner screen of S.C. boats, but no damage was caused. A little later the *Brooklyn,* tracked two groups of aircraft thought to be hostile, but which did not approach the beaches though they searched the "Camel" fire support area for nearly an hour. The *Nevada* returned to the assault area on the 19th, and the bombardment of Porquerolles and of positions near Hyères was resumed. The *Quincy* fired 147 rounds at the island batteries and the *Omaha* 24, while the *Quincy* also supported the *Georges Leygues,* which carried out a bombardment against troops who were trying to hold Hyères against the French, and also against batteries and strong points in the same neighbourhood.

On 20th August, the port of St. Raphael was opened. It had been planned, to open the beaches in Hyères Roads and to extend those at Le Lavandou, but the advance of the army had been so rapid and unloading so satisfactory that it was decided to cancel this plan. The bombardment of Porquerolles was continued on a reduced scale on the 20th by the *Philadelphia, Emile Bertin, Le Malin* and *Le Fantasque,* but heavy bombardments were carried out against the Giens batteries and against positions north-east and south of Hyères, by the *Black Prince, Emile Bertin, Philadelphia, Augusta,* and the French destroyers. The *Philadelphia,* was the most heavily engaged, firing 281 rounds during the day, and the *Augusta* 114. The *Black Prince* demolished the Golf Hotel, an important enemy observation post near Hyères.

So far the weather had been ideal, but on 21st August, strong easterly winds caused a choppy sea with swell and surf on the beaches and the following day the sea was sufficiently high to impede unloading. On the 23rd the weather was again fine but the warning had been given that autumn was approaching, with the probability of gales which would render beach work impossible. It was urgent to open a major port without delay; fortunately, Toulon and Marseilles were soon to fall.

During the early hours of the 21st three E-Boats tried to penetrate the screen off the Lerins Islands, and two were promptly sunk by the destroyers but the third escaped for a time, though she was located by cruiser aircraft at 0400 and sunk by a destroyer.[2] "Delta"

1 H. diagram 21.
2 H. pp. 70, 71. On p. 69, however, it is said that one enemy was sunk, one driven ashore and one damaged.

Red and Green beaches were closed down on the 21st. The action against Porquerolles continued, the *Eberle* firing 160 rounds on the 21st, and the *Lorraine* 11 from her heavy guns, while the *Emile Bertin* and the French destroyers engaged the Giens positions.

In the afternoon the *Eberle* sighted a small group of men waving a white flag on the south-west point of the island; a boat was sent in and a number of Armenians, who had fled from the German stronghold, surrendered.

34.

Next day, 22nd, the bombardment was continued by the *Montcalm,* which fired nearly 100 rounds and the Germans finally surrendered. In the evening the *Hackberry* landed a company of Senegalese troops to garrison the island and came under fire from batteries on the Giens Peninsula.[1] The bombardment of the Giens batteries was continued on the 22nd by the *Philadelphia,* which fired 282 rounds, supported by the *Omaha, Montcalm, Georges Leygues,* and *Le Malin,* and though some batteries were silenced resistance continued till dusk. Plans were made for an intensive bombardment next day, but in the morning white flags were seen to be flying ashore and a party sent in to reconnoitre found that the Germans had evacuated the Peninsula. The entire area of the Hyères Roads were now free of the enemy, and ships engaged in bombarding the Toulon defences could shelter under the lee of Glens.

On the 22nd Admiral Hewitt released the *Ajax, Argonaut, Orion,* seven "Hunt" class destroyers and all the British L.S.I. to C.-in-C. Mediterranean.

On the 23rd a new P.T. boat patrol was established off Nice and Villefranche to guard against explosive boats and further E-Boat attacks, and next day patrol vessels broke up by gunfire what was probably an attempt to launch an attack by explosive boats or human torpedoes from Antibes. The night P.T. patrol to the westward of Hyères Roads was now discontinued, the threat from Toulon being judged inconsiderable.

A number of vessels were released from the operation on the 24th. Next day the *Sirius* arrived and relieved the *Aurora* while on the 26th Admiral Hewitt released the *Arkansas, Nevada, Texas* and a number of other vessels.

On the 25th the screen thwarted an explosive boat attack from the Nice area, and though the destroyers and P.Ts. avoided damage to themselves from numerous explosions, they were not successful in hitting any of the enemy, but next night when the enemy renewed the attempt with ten controlled explosive boats, eight of them were destroyed by the *Livermore* and P.T. *552,* though the control boat unfortunately escaped. On the 26th the destroyers *Gleaves, Niblack* and *Benson* made a sweep up the coast as far as Spezia in an attempt to intercept two enemy destroyers which had been reported at sea. The "Alpha" sector was now extended to include the Hyères Islands, but the gunfire support ships engaged in this area remained under the command of Admiral Davidson. On the 27th Admiral Hewitt ordered that convoy escorts should be reduced by half, subject to a minimum of two, and on this day a continuous L.C.V.P. patrol in "Camel" area against human torpedoes was instituted. On the 27th also, three small enemy craft

1 H. p. 220 says that the final bombardment of Porquerolles was by the Aurora, Philadelphia and Lorraine, but diagram 21 shows the Philadelphia engaged with the Glens forts and the other two ships bombarding Toulon. Aurora's R. of P. (M011228/44) shows that the ship was for a time stationed off Porquerolles, but makes no mention of firing at the island. Admiral Hewitt's report (H. p. 72) says that the Omaha accepted the surrender of the island at 1130, but diagram 21 of the report shows that the Montcalrn' s bombardment took place at 1541.

were captured; one a fishing vessel containing the entire crew of a U-Boat, which had run aground off Toulon and had been destroyed to avoid capture, was making for Genoa; the other two boats contained Germans who were trying to escape from Toulon, and were also heading for Italy.

Admiral Hewitt released the *Omaha, Cincinnatti, Marblehead* and *Stuart Prince* on the 27th, and the *Termagant, Terpsichore* and *Quincy* on the 28th. On 28th August, both Toulon and Marseilles surrendered, thus bringing to a close the second phase of Operation "Dragoon".

35. The Seizure of Port de Bono

By 23rd August, the 6th Corps was moving swiftly up the Rhône Valley and the problem of supplies for these troops as well as for the French Army corps moving against Toulon and Marseilles caused some anxiety. It was not expected that the two great ports would be able to make a long resistance but it was feared that the German demolitions would be such as to render the ports almost useless for weeks, while with the approach of autumn it was certain that unloading over the beaches would suffer frequent delays owing to bad weather. Accordingly it was decided to open the Gulf of Fos in order to provide an entry into Port de Bouc and the Etang de Berre. The low flat country north of Port de Bouc was ideal for establishing airfields while the port was well situated to receive the fuel and supplies necessary to operate the air forces. Reports had been received that the Germans had evacuated the town and that the area was under the control of the F.F.I. (Resistance Movement) and French Commandos. The Port could be developed to take five or six cargo ships while large tankers could berth in the petroleum basins and there were ample facilities for the storage of fuel. Port de Bouc was connected with Arles by a canal which was navigable for L.C.M. though blocked by fallen bridges, and another short canal led into the Etang de Berre, which would be used as an anchorage by medium sized cargo ships.

Admiral Davidson was given charge of the operations for opening the port. The work of the minesweepers in opening up the port under fire from batteries in the Marseilles area has already been described in section 44. On 26th August, an advance naval party was landed and on 27th August, a channel into the port was clear, so L.S.T. *134* arrived to commence salvage operations followed by several pontoon causeways, tugs and boom vessels. Before nightfall the inner harbour was reported ready to receive a cargo vessel drawing up to 22 feet and a tanker with a draught of 26 feet. The principal salvage work necessary to clear the port for large scale operation was the raising or moving of four ships sunk in some of the berths, filling in a number of craters, and removing or restoring five large cranes which were obstructing the principal quay.

The entrance to the Arles canal was blocked by a line of concrete pyramids, but these had already been partly cleared by the French, though it was necessary to clear three bridges, twisted masses of steel which blocked the canal between the port and Arles and also two spans of the railway bridge near Martigues, which were obstructing the entrance to the Etang de Berre. No mines were found in the port, but as late as 5th September, an explosion occurred while a French tug was berthing the American salvage vessel *Tackle;* the tug was sunk and the American ship was badly damaged. After this the port was closed for 48 hours but still no mines were found. It was thought that a solitary mine was attached to a buoy which the tug grazed. The canals were soon opened and on 1st

September, fourteen L.C.M. from the combat loaders *Procyon* and *Arcturus* were able to proceed up the Rhône to Arles, where for a week they worked twenty-four hours a day ferrying French troops across the river.

On 28th August, when Toulon and Marseilles fell, it was found that the damage to the ports was less than expected and the majority of the salvage parties were diverted from Port de Bouc, the importance of which was reduced. The port was then principally used for the discharge and storage of fuel. By 25th September, three berths for Liberty ships and one for tankers had been cleared which sufficed for an auxiliary unloading port. It was decided not to use the Etang de Berre owing to the difficulty of clearing the wreckage of the railway bridge. By 25th September, over 30,000 tons of cargo and 240,000 barrels of fuel had been discharged at Port de Bouc; the cargo alone represented 10% of that unloaded over the beaches up to this date and 25% of that unloaded through the ports, while the fuel amounted to 70% of the total amount discharged at all points[1] so that the opening of this port had a considerable influence on the successful progress of the invasion.

36. The Reduction of Toulon

The great naval base of Toulon was surrounded by batteries, with the heaviest concentration guarding the seaward approaches. Cape Sicié to the west of the St. Mandrier Peninsula had at least thirteen guns with a range of 18,000 yards, while the peninsula itself, which guards Toulon harbour and its approaches and was the key point of the whole seaward defensive system, mounted no less than seventy guns of which half had a range of at least 18,000 yards. Two of these batteries, which consisted of twin-mounted 13.4-inch guns taken from the old battleship *Provence,* proved to be a serious obstacle to our gun support ships as they outranged all our guns.[2] The northern shore of Toulon Bay was much less heavily defended but there were batteries along this coast, the heaviest of which was one of four 5.5-inch guns on Carqueiranne Point. The outer defences consisted of the guns on the Giens Peninsula and Porquerolles Island.

Naval operations against Toulon opened on 19th August, when Admiral Davidson in the *Augusta,* with the *Nevada* and *Lorraine,* escorted by the *Kearney, Ericsson, Eberle* and *Gleaves,* carried out a bombardment of the St. Mandrier positions and of Toulon harbour to test the strength of the defences. Aerial spotting was employed and the ships were screened with smoke. The *Nevada* fired 125 rounds, one of her targets being the *Strasbourg,* on which she scored a direct hit, the *Lorraine* fired 59 rounds and the *Augusta* 27. The return fire from the enemy batteries was not heavy, possibly because this bombardment followed a heavy air raid. By the 20th, the French Army had encircled Toulon and on this day bombardment of the shore batteries was carried out from 0730 to 1820. The *Quincy* was heavily engaged, firing 524 rounds[3] while the *Georges Leygues* fired 162; of the battleships, the *Nevada* fired 117 rounds and the *Lorraine* 76; the destroyers *Le Fantasque* and *Mc.Cook* also joined in the bombardment. The *Georges Leygues* and *Le Fantasque* were both hit by six-inch shells, but no serious damage was sustained. British ships took little part in this action, but the *Lookout* fired 116 rounds and the *Aurora* 12. In general air spotting was employed though the *Georges Leygues* and the destroyers sometimes approached the shore sufficiently to spot their own fall of shot. The enemy made a spirited reply to this

1 H. p. 225.
2 H. p. 220.
3 Details of bombardments are from H. diagrams 21 and 22.

prolonged attack, and the operations were dominated by the two 13.4-inch batteries which appeared to have a range of 34,000 yards.[1] Captain Barnard of the *Aurora* remarked in his report that although the chances of a 13.4-inch shell hitting a cruiser at medium range were theoretically very small, the large splashes from these shells falling within four cables of the ship produced an uncomfortable feeling, and he felt lonely within 18,000 to 20,000 yards of the heavy batteries without a smoke screening destroyer.[2] The *Aurora's* fire was to have been spotted by forward observation, but although she remained in position for several hours, communication with the observer was very bad and there were numerous delays, with the result that the ship was only able to fire twelve rounds. Finally, the enemy's fire became so heavy and accurate that the *Aurora* had to withdraw under cover of smoke laid by *Le Malin.* Captain Bernard reported to Admiral Davidson that he considered it an unreasonable risk to use a cruiser close inshore in these circumstances without a screening destroyer and a counter battery ship.

The naval bombardment on this day was backed up by two attacks by medium bombers, which dropped 139 tons of bombs on the St. Mandrier forts this was the last air attack on the Toulon fortifications. Admiral Hewitt remarks that further aerial attacks would have been useful at this time, but the tactical situation was such that the entire strength of the Air Force was required to support the infantry advance in the north and destroy the retreating enemy road convoys.[3] A Commando operation to destroy the heavy batteries on St. Mandrier was considered but it was decided that this would not be feasible without much heavier air support than was available, and the ships had to continue the attack without other aid than that given by the army artillery. On 21st August, there was a lull in the operations against Toulon, though ships were engaged both with the Porquerolles and Giens forts and with the outer defences of Marseilles, but the *Lorraine* fired some fifty rounds against the St Mandrier and Carqueiranne batteries and the *Emile Bertin* was also in action. On the following day the *Aurora* and *Quincy* were engaged against the Toulon defences firing 108 and 172 rounds respectively, while the *Lorraine* and the *Georges Leygues* also fired a few rounds and the *Montcalm* fired about 150 rounds against guns and strong points about half way between Hyères and Toulon and near the main road.

The *Aurora* again had communication troubles with her spotter, on this occasion an aircraft, and once more came under fairly heavy fire from the 13.4-inch guns, but she was well screened by the *Eberle,* though at times owing to variations in wind "the *Aurora* gave a good representation of an ostrich with her posterior sticking out of the smoke."[4] On this day the ship, when south of Porquerolles Island, was fired at by the heavy St. Mandrier batteries at a range of over 30,000 yards, and later in the day when engaging a battery on Cape Brun the *Aurora* and *Eberle* were under continuous fire from the same batteries for forty minutes, shells falling as near as two cables from the *Aurora.* At this juncture the *Eberle* reported that her smoke was nearly exhausted, but the *Ericsson* was speedily sent to relieve her. The *Aurora's* shoot was successful, for according to the spotting aircraft the ship registered eight hits inside the fort, including two direct hits on the guns.[5] It was on this day that, as related in *Section* 34, Porquerolles surrendered and the Germans evacuated the Giens Peninsula, under whose lee gunfire support ships operating against Toulon could

1 M01128/44 R. of P. Aurora p. 1.
2 M011228/44 p. 1 and end. A. p. 1.
3 H. p. 221.
4 M011228/44 R. of P. Aurora p. 3.
5 M011228/44 R. of P. Aurora p. 3.

now shelter. On 23rd August, the weight of the attack against Toulon was considerably increased, and the bombardment continued from, 0945 till 1745. The *Nevada* fired 282 rounds, the *Lorraine* 57, the *Montcalm* and *Georges Leygues* each fired 285 rounds, the *Gloire* 173 and the *Quincy* 136. The *Aurora* was engaged with a battery south of Hyères, which surrendered after the bombardment. On the 24th the battleships were not engaged with the Toulon forts but the *Gloire* in a series of bombardments fired 677 rounds the *Georges Leygues* 282 and the *Aurora* 226, while the *Quincy* and the *Plunkett,* were less heavily engaged; the firing was mostly directed by shore fire control parties. The shore observer, who was spotting for the *Aurora,* reported that the first rounds were always near the map reference given, the spread was very small for line and about 300 yards for range, and the shoots were the best which he had seen.[1]

37.

It had been determined to make a concentrated effort on 25th August to force the surrender of the St. Mandrier forts by an intense bombardment. In the absence of Admiral Davidson in the *Augusta,* who with most of the American ships was engaged in supporting the minesweepers in Marseilles Bay, Captain Barnard of the *Aurora* was ordered to take command of the bombarding force in spite of the fact that he was the junior captain, and that Rear-Admiral Jaujard, commanding the French ships, was present.[2] It should be noted, however, that the *Ramillies, Sirius* and *Omaha* were not present at the beginning of the day, so that apart from the French officers Captain Barnard was the senior officer on the spot. It is not stated why this unusual arrangement was made and it is evident that Captain Barnard was not informed of it in advance, for, up to 0058 of the 25th when he received orders from Admiral Davidson to assign targets to the force, he had thought himself under Admiral Jaujard's orders; in the words of an Admiralty comment on Captain Barnard's report, however, his task "was both effectively and tactfully carried out" in spite of his invidious position. The bombarding squadron consisted of the *Ramillies, Lorraine, Aurora, Sirius, Omaha, Montcalm, Gloire, Georges Leygues, Lookout, Kendrick* and *Le Fantasque,* but the *Ramillies, Sirius* and *Omaha* only arrived during the afternoon.

Captain Barnard had formed the opinion that the batteries which remained active could either be destroyed, or so neutralised that the Army could capture them, within a period of twelve hours of daylight. Captain Barnard's plan was to station an outer ring of counter battery ships in Hyères Roads and two or three heavy ships to the south of Toulon Bay. Further inshore would be stationed some quick hitting ships, light cruisers or French heavy destroyers, whose role would be to act as bait and provoke the enemy batteries; each of these bombardment ships would be attached to a separate shore fire control party. An inner ring of fleet destroyers would have the primary duty of keeping the light cruisers screened with smoke, but the destroyers would be free to emerge from the smoke in turn and fire rapid salvos at any active battery. When it appeared that the more dangerous batteries had been silenced, the smoke screens would be discontinued and all ships would close to secondary armament range and keep up a heavy direct fire until the Army was ready to mop up the enemy in his dug-outs.[3]

1 MO11228/44 R. of P. Aurora p. 6.
2 H. p. 221. M011228/44 R. of P. Aurora. Encl.A. Part 2 pp. 1, 2.
3 M011228 R, of P. Aurora. Encl.A. Part 2 p.1.

The plan was not entirely successful for the collapse of the enemy was not brought about during the day, but on the other hand Captain Barnard's force did not attain the strength which he had visualised, and the *Aurora,* far from acting mainly as "bait" took a much greater part in the bombardment than any other ship. By daylight on the 25th the greater part of the town of Toulon had been occupied by French troops, but the St. Mandrier peninsula was holding out. Captain Barnard in the *Aurora* with the *Lorraine,* screened by the *Lookout* and *Kendrick,* took station south of Porquerolles at 0700, where they were later joined by the *Montcalm* and *Le Fantasque.* The *Gloire* and *Georges Leygues* were stationed inside Hyères Roads. There was difficulty in finding out the exact position ashore and in obtaining contact with the Army, so that firing did not start until 0928 when the *Gloire* commenced bombarding with a shore fire control party spotting. The *Lorraine* opened fire on one of the heavy batteries at 1204 with air spotting, and shortly after the *Aurora* also opened fire. The enemy's heavy batteries replied but the fire does not seem to have been very heavy. The action then became general and the *Omaha* joined in the firing at 1422, but the *Georges Leygues* was detached from the squadron and apparently did not open fire. The bombarding ships moved to the westward and entered Toulon Bay and before 1300 Captain Barnard was able to report to Admiral Davidson that the *Lorraine* had put the two heavy batteries out of action, but 6-inch batteries were still firing at our ships. During the afternoon the bombardment increased in intensity and the *Aurora* was almost continuously engaged. Admiral Davidson's general orders had assigned the *Aurora's* support as "lee of Giens," but with an easterly wind blowing, Captain Barnard interpreted this somewhat freely as giving him liberty of action in Toulon Bay. The *Ramillies,* which was on her way from Propriano to Algiers when in the evening of the 24th she received orders to proceed to the assault area, arrived off Porquerolles at 1400; she had received no other instructions until she arrived within visual signalling distance of the bombarding ships,[1] and even then did not entirely understand the situation; she opened fire at 1640 but ceased after firing sixteen rounds as the target was invisible owing to smoke. In spite of a signal from the *Aurora* asking for utmost fire, the *Ramillies* was not able to recommence the bombardment until 1838, and this time she scored several hits on a battery.

At 1555 the *Sirius* arrived, and opened fire with commendable rapidity. Meanwhile Admiral Davidson was planning for a concentrated bombardment from 1800 to 1900, and Captain Barriard, on receiving the orders, believed that the Army was to attack at 1900 when the barrage lifted. The bombardment continued and at 1825 all ships were ordered to cease making smoke so as to give a clear view for direct fire. The *Lorraine* was hotly engaged with her main and secondary armament and at 1840 her fire caused two heavy explosions, apparently magazines blowing up, and the *Ramillies* silenced two batteries. Captain Barnard alludes several times to the efficiency of the *Lorraine* and the accuracy of her fire. By 1850 there was no sign of life on the peninsula, and at 1900 the "Cease Fire" was ordered. At this juncture the *Simoun* arrived wearing the flag of Vice-Admiral Lemonnier, Chief of the French Naval Staff. This ship paid no attention to the cease fire signal, and opened fire,[2] being with difficulty restrained from carrying out a private bombardment.

1 M011587/44 R. of P. Ramillies.
2 M011228 R. of P. Aurora p. 3.

Soon after 1900 the squadron retired for the night and the *Aurora* sailed from the area after receiving commendatory signals from Rear-Admirals Davidson and Jaujard. During the day the *Aurora* had fired 904 rounds, the *Montcalm* 321, the *Gloire* 149, the *Omaha* 169, and the *Sirius* 130. Of the battleships the *Lorraine* fired 102 rounds and the *Ramillies* 62; the *Lookout's* score was 411, and that of the *Kendrick* 117 while the *Fantasque* fired 47 rounds. It is not clear if an assault by the Army at 1900 was really intended, but it was not carried out, though a summons to surrender was issued by the Army. Captain Barnard considered that all batteries had been neutralised by 1900 and that the whole position could have been captured had all the ships landed their marines.

Bombardment was reopened at 1300 on 26th August, and between then and 1645 the *Montcalm* fired 731 rounds, the *Gloire* 632, the *Lorraine* 293, the *Fantasque* 241, the *Sirius* 93, the *Kendrick* 64, and the *Ramillies* 35.[1] The *Ramillies* scored some hits on batteries and observed no retaliatory fire, but St. Mandrier still would not surrender though Fort Six-Fours on the Cape Sicié peninsula capitulated during the day. On the 27th the *Ramillies* again opened fire at 1053 and fired 48 rounds of which 34 fell within 50 yards of the target and several were reported as direct hits;[2] the *Duguay Trouin* also fired 67 rounds, and after some negotiations Rear-Admiral Ruhfus surrendered St. Mandrier next day with about 2,000 men. Toulon and all the other defences had for some time been occupied by the French Army.

After the capture of St. Mandrier it was found that the enemy personnel in the deep underground spaces had been completely protected from bombs and shells, but surface communications were badly damaged and many gun positions had been put out of action. The ground near the two 13.4-inch turrets was ploughed by bombs and naval gunfire. One of the turrets was hit, probably by a bomb, but this turret had already been put out of action by sabotage or accident, and it is not believed that it was in action during, the operations. The nozzle of the left gun of the other turret had been hit by a large fragment which put the gun out of action, but the right gun was serviceable up to the time of the surrender.[3]

38. The Clearance of Toulon Harbour

As Toulon and Marseilles fell simultaneously the Army modified its plan for port clearance and decided to use all forces available for the clearance of Marseilles to the exclusion of Toulon. This decision was due to the fact that the re-opening of rail outlets from Toulon would take a considerable time, while Marseilles had a far greater number of berths, and it was considered that the personnel and equipment available were only sufficient to work one port at a time.[4] Admiral Hewitt, however, decided that the development of all possible protected unloading berths was of the greatest importance, and as surveys showed that some berths could be provided at Toulon long before any at Marseilles would be ready, he determined to open Toulon as a purely naval operation. Five pontoon causeway platoons were transferred from the beaches to Toulon, followed later by the four platoons from Port de Bouc. The port area of Toulon was badly damaged, both by

1 These figures are taken from H. Diagram 21. Admiral Hewitt (H., p. 221) implies that there was no bombardment on the 26th or 27th, but the R. of P. of Ramillies (MO11587/44) shows that she was engaged, and the Lorraine and the French cruisers were also in action.

2 M011587 R. of P. Ramillies encl. 2. p. 3.

3 H. p. 285.

4 H. p. 340.

our intensive bombing and by German demolitions. Almost all buildings in the port had been demolished, the roads blocked and torn up, the docks damaged, and most of the berths obstructed by scuttled ships.

With limited equipment and no land crane facilities, debris was cleared, roads opened, dock areas levelled, wrecks bridged to provide unloading berths, and ramps built up to the roofs of dock structures to provide access for trucks to otherwise useless berths. A large wrecked swing bridge had to be cut up and removed from the channel leading to some of the inner basin berths. Materials such as lumber, spikes, welding and cutting gases were procured through local French naval and civilian agencies, since no provision had been made by the American Navy, which had not expected to be made responsible for the operation, and it was remarkable in the circumstances that so much material should have been available. The Navy Salvage Groups co-operated fully with the construction battalions and a great amount of ingenuity on the part of the construction battalion (Seabee) personnel overcame many obstacles, especially the lack of cranes. Prisoners of War were used extensively and French dockyard workmen followed up and improved the initial rough developments. No attempt was made to perform any work that did not contribute to the earliest availability of unloading berths.[1]

The work was started on 4th September, and next day a Liberty ship was able to berth alongside, while a second berth was available on the 6th, thus fully justifying Admiral Hewitt's decision to open the port, for at Marseilles no berths were available until the 15th. By the 25th of the month nine berths alongside for Liberty ships and thirty-one bow on berths for L.C.T. were available,[2] and the Army was using Toulon for landing troops, civilian supplies and motor transport. Up to 25th September, 5,085 troops had been disembarked as well as 2,628 vehicles and over 100,000 ton's of stores.[3]

39. The Capture of Marseilles

There is less information about the operations against the Marseilles area than about Toulon, mainly because no British major units were engaged. The defences of Marseilles were much less formidable than those of Toulon. The inner defences consisted of batteries on the islands of Ratonneau, Pomègues and If, in Marseilles Bay, and five batteries on Cape Croisette, the heaviest of which appears to have been one of four 5.5-inch guns. The outer defences extended south westward from Cape Croisette as far as Ile des Embiez off the Cape Sicié Peninsula, and included batteries round the Bay of La Ciotat and Sanary Bay and on Embiez Island. The La Ciotat batteries had been attacked from the air on 13th and 14th August, and were not engaged by the naval forces. There were also some batteries along the coast between Marseilles and the Gulf of Fos, notably at Cape Méjean and Cape Couronne, which as mentioned in Section 44 were engaged by ships protecting the minesweepers, which were employed in sweeping a channel through the Gulf, to open up Port de Bouc.

On 20th August, the batteries on the Ile d'Embiez were engaged by the *Nevada*, which fired 50 rounds,[4] *Quincy* and *McCook*. The *Nevada* also fired 70 rounds at a battery near Bandol and the *Quincy* fired a few rounds at another battery near Sanary-sur-Mer,

1 H. p. 341.
2 H. p. 230.
3 H. p. 341.
4 H. Diagram 22.

supported by *Le Fantasque* which fired 45 rounds. On the 21st and 23rd the *Quincy* again bombarded batteries overlooking Sanary Bay, firing in all 139 rounds. There were no further bombardments in this neighbourhood so presumably the batteries were put out of action. On 22nd August, the *Augusta* fired 54 rounds at a railway crossing on the outskirts of Marseilles. On 24th August, the minesweepers arrived to commence sweeping a channel into Marseilles and the gun support ships commenced the reduction of the inner defences. The *Nevada* fired 143 rounds at batteries on the three islands in Marseilles Bay, and on the next three days these batteries were attacked from the air, 303 tons of bombs being dropped on them, after which they received no further attention from naval guns. On the 25th the *Augusta* bombarded batteries in the neighbourhood of Cape Croisette, giving direct support to the minesweepers. She fired 336 rounds during the day and was supported and screened by the *Livermore* and *Ludlow,* which joined in the bombardment when opportunity offered. On the 26th the *Augusta* fired another 63 rounds at the same targets, while on the 27th the only battery remaining active was heavily engaged by the *Madison,* which fired 280 rounds. Admiral Hewitt says that the *Quincy* and *Philadelphia* also joined in these bombardments,[1] but they are not mentioned in the detailed diagram No. 22 of his report.

The Army, greatly helped by the F.F.I., quickly penetrated the land defences of Marseilles and the town was captured on the 28th, the same day as Toulon fell, but extended negotiations were required before the islands would surrender as the garrisons declared that they would continue to resist if required to submit to the French. Eventually, on 29th August, the Captain of the *Philadelphia* landed on Ratonneau Island with a detachment of marines, and accepted the surrender of the German forces. This action was taken to avoid further delay in opening the way for the minesweepers.

At Marseilles, contrary to what happened at Toulon, the work of clearance, apart of course from minesweeping, devolved on the Army and the only contribution of the Navy was eight bull-dozers with their crews and the provision of electric power in the port by two submarines. On 1st September, the Army requested that Seabees should be transferred from Toulon but eventually withdrew the demand.[2] The first two berths were ready on 15th September, and three days later there were eleven alongside berths available and a further eleven holding berths. By 25th September, clearance had proceeded so well that there were 16 berths alongside for Liberty ships as well as 23 holding berths and 45 berths, bows on, for L.C.T.

40. Naval Gun Support on Right Flank

Naval forces gave gunfire support to the right flank of the Army throughout the operation. The bombardments during the first three days have been mentioned in Section 35, while the advance of the Army as far as the Italian frontier, where it was held up, is dealt with in *Section* 24. On 18th August, the *Brooklyn, Tuscaloosa,* with the destroyers *Edison, Woolsey* and *Boyle,* bombarded batteries near Cannes in most cases spotting being from the firing ship. The *Brooklyn* was the most heavily engaged, firing over 200 rounds.[3] The enemy's return fire did no damage. In the course of the day some ships of the force penetrated into La Napoule Gulf, without drawing any fire.

1 H. p. 221.
2 H. p. 341.
3 H. Diagram 20.

During the following days the bombardments continued, the targets including besides batteries, troops, vehicles, and supply dumps. The *Brooklyn* continued to take the principal part in these operations. On the 22nd two destroyers were hit and suffered casualties while firing at a battery in the Gulf of La Napoule. On this day the *Champlin* arrived to augment the bombarding force and on the 23rd the bombardment was increased in intensity to support the advance of the airborne division on Cannes, which town, together with Antibes, fell on the 24th, when the bombarding ships moved further along the coast.

On 25th and 26th August, the *Woolsey, Edison, Boyle* and *Champlin,* together with the *Emile Bertin* and *Le Terrible,* supported the Allied advance towards Nice by bombarding targets in the neighbourhood of Cagnes.[1] On the 27th our land forces crossed the Var and the ships engaged targets near Nice and on Cape Ferrat; three enemy minesweepers at Villfranche were destroyed. Nice fell on the 28th. On 30th August, after a two-day lull, the *Edison* and *Woolsey* bombarded guns, vehicles, and strong points near Monaco, and were under fire from an enemy battery which they were not able to silence. During the first three days of September the same destroyers continued to fire, extending operations as far as Cape Martin. On 4th September, the airborne troops were fighting hard on a line running from Sospel to Monaco and the *Ludlow* and *Le Malin* gave support, firing at targets inland as well as on the coast: the *Ludlow* fired close on 500 rounds during the day. Next day the *Montcalm* also was engaged and fired over 400 rounds, while *Le Malin* bombarded concrete emplacements to the north of Sospel and the *Ludlow* again was active. During the day the *Ludlow* and *Le Malin* were attacked by human torpedoes without receiving any damage; the destroyers sank three torpedoes rescuing three survivors. Bombardments in the Monaco and Sospel areas continued until 9th September, the *Duguay Trouin* and *H. P. Jones* augmenting the Support Force. Shortly before midnight of 7th to 8th September the gunfire support destroyers were attacked by explosive boats in a position five miles south of Cape St. Ampeglio, but succeeded in avoiding damage and sank two of the boats, while P.T. boats accounted for four or five more; the control boat unfortunately escaped.

On 9th September, the enemy launched a counter-attack against our troops near Castillon, about six miles north of Cape Martin. The *H. P. Jones* opened a heavy fire on the enemy, and after the destroyer had fired 720 rounds and had destroyed several tanks, the attack was repulsed. Later in the day another counter-attack was delivered by the Germans from the neighbourhood of Mount Bellenda, and again the *H. P. Jones* was prominent in the defeat of the enemy's effort. The shore fire control party reported that the ship's fire had inflicted heavy casualties on the enemy.[2] The *Duguay Trouin,* which bombarded Bordighera, and the *Madison,* also took part in the day's firing. Next morning the Germans launched a human torpedo attack on the fire support ships. At least ten of these torpedoes were sunk, mainly by the *Madison* and *Woolsey.* The attacks went on from dawn till noon but hardly interfered with the bombardments which were carried out against the Bellenda area and to the east of Cape St. Ampeglio.

On 11th September, the enemy launched a counter-attack against our troops near Menton, which was broken up largely by the efforts of the *Ludlow* and *Woolsey,* each of which fired over 400 rounds; in addition, the human torpedoes launching base at

1 H. Diagram 23.
2 H. p. 107

Ventimiglia was bombarded, while the *Lorraine* fired 150 rounds with her heavy guns against fortifications near Castillon, the spotting aircraft reporting four hits. On the 13th our troops were east of Menton, and henceforth bombardments were mainly directed on targets between Cape Mortola and Cape St. Ampeglio, but on the 14th the *Ludlow* fired 150 rounds into Oneglio harbour hitting two ships, while the *Edison* hit and damaged a vessel off Cape Cervo. On 15th September, two destroyers attempted to bombard the harbour at Imperia, where aircraft had reported several ships, but a shore battery prevented the destroyers from approaching. Besides bombarding shore positions, the destroyers had to afford protection to the minesweepers, which were clearing a channel along the coast.

Several bombardments were carried out on points well inside the Italian frontier, and on the 18th the *H. P. Jones* fired at San Remo from 0700 to 0940 and for an expenditure of 223 rounds silenced an anti-aircraft battery, destroyed two E-boats, blew up two ammunition dumps and three ammunition barges besides destroying or damaging six or seven other craft. The destroyer's captain attributed his success largely to the pilot of the spotting aircraft, a seaplane from the *Philadelphia*.[1] Leaving San Remo harbour ablaze the *H. P. Jones* proceeded to Porto Maurizio at which she fired 250 rounds between 1700 and 1800, sinking three vessels and damaging five more besides setting fuel tanks and ammunition dumps on fire.[2] The destroyers continued to bombard the Ventimiglia area up to 25th September, when Operation "Dragoon" came to an end. The Army did not succeed in making any appreciable advance until the final collapse of Germany in May, 1945. Gunfire support continued to be given by the Allied Navies, but this responsibility eventually devolved upon the Flag Officer Western Italy.

41. Naval Events in Assault Area. 29th August to 25th September

The disembarkation of troops and vehicles, and the unloading of stores over the beaches continued at a very satisfactory rate, and the convoy programme was maintained and at times accelerated. On 5th September, arrangements were made to speed up the troop lift by two L.S.T. ferry services. One was to run between the assault area and Naples with a total number of 24 to 26 L.S.T, and the other was to operate between Oran and the assault area with from 25 to 27 ships. After the 14th the Oran service was augmented by ten L.S.T. which had been engaged on a shuttle service between Calvi and the beaches, for the benefit of the Air Force. As in all amphibious operations the greater part of the unloading was accomplished by small craft, and mainly by 130 L.C.T., 200 L.C.M. and the D.U.K.W.S. The Army was responsible for the D.U.K.W.S., but the other unloading craft together with numerous P.C., and S.C. boats, Y.M.S., P.Ts., and small tugs required logistic support, the provision of which was always a problem; the presence of Mother Ships however, greatly simplified the task of maintaining these craft and their crews, who in the nature of things were very hard worked.

In each assault area there was one American L.S.T. Mother Ship and one or two British L.C.I. Mother Craft. In addition to providing berthing, messing, repair facilities, fuel and water, these ships carried maximum quantities of provisions, canteen stores, clothing, lubricating oil, smoke pots and other consumable supplies. The ships were also

1 H. p. 286.
2 H. p. 121.

equipped to provide medical attention and recreational facilities for the crews of the small craft. Each L.S.T. was fitted with 150 portable bunks, two 625 cubit foot refrigerators and one portable distilling set. The L.C.I. were less well equipped, but no more than three L.S.T. could be spared. As an example of work carried out by these L.S.T. the following figures may be quoted for L.S.T. 74 covering the period between D-day and noon on 8th September.[1]

Ships and Craft watered and fuelled	225
Water issued	552 tons
Fuel issued	945 tons
Fog oil issued	200 drums
Smoke pots and floats issued	1,752
Ships and Craft repaired	109
Patients treated	76
Ships and Craft provisioned	194
Fresh provisions issued	64 tons
Dry provisions issued	132 tons
Average daily berthing	256
Average daily rations	307

Admiral Hewitt remarks that L.S.D. would be more suitable for this work than L.S.T., but only two of these were available for the operation, and they were fully engaged in transporting small craft and pontoon causeways during the maintenance period, and it was impossible to use them as Mother ships.[2]

In previous operations it had often been difficult for landing craft and boats to find the ships to which they were ordered to proceed, but this time arrangements had been made for ships to fly special distinguishing flags at the yardarm, and colliers, tankers and water barges always had a flag hoist flying to indicate the quantity of coal, fuel, or water remaining on hand for discharge. Merchant ships in convoys were assigned numbers, and these numbers were painted on large sign-boards secured to each side of the ship, and were at night illuminated by low visibility lights. Experiments were also made with luminous paint and luminous tape.[3] The result of all these measures was that ships could rapidly be identified by day or night, and boats did not have to waste hours in searching for ships, as sometimes happened at Salerno.

42.

In anticipation of bad weather after the beginning of September, comprehensive storm plans had been evolved for each sector. Landing craft of all types are particularly vulnerable to gale damage by reason of their high freeboard and small draught, and the plans dealt mainly with the safety of these craft, problems of craft beached, at anchor, and under way being treated separately. Special attention was paid to D.U.K.W.S., which are particularly liable to damage by rough seas, and to pontoon causeways, which are almost impossible to

1 H. p. 325.
2 H. p. 325.
3 H. p. 336.

salvage if they have been broached.[1] On several occasions during the operation unloading operations were curtailed by bad weather, but only one storm of real intensity struck the assault area. During the afternoon of 2nd September, the wind, from the north-west, increased in strength and by 2100 the wind speed was 30 knots; a violent mistral of 45 knots with gusts up to 60 knots had arisen by 0200 of the 3rd, falling to 30 knots by noon and to 15 knots by nightfall. During the 2nd the sea at the beaches was not high enough to stop boat work, though unloading was slowed down and all P.T. boat patrols were cancelled and all minesweeping abandoned. During the night there were heavy seas on the beaches, but unloading was resumed in the morning. So well had the storm plans been conceived that only one L.C.M. and one L.C.V.P. were sunk and two S.C. boats, three L.C.V.P. and four L.C.M. damaged.[2]

As time went on Admiral Hewitt was able to release ships from the assault area, and his forces progressively decreased in strength. On 29th August, the *Ramillies* and the two American Carriers were released followed on the 30th by the *Sirius, Dido,* and *Tuscaloosa.* By 1st September, all air control facilities were in full working order ashore and the last of the air control ships, F.D.T.13, was released. On 4th September, an air raid was carried out against Genoa, during the course of which the destroyer *Squadrista,* one torpedo boat, five submarines and three escort vessels were sunk.

On 5th September, all naval activities at Propriano came to an end, and the following day Admiral Hewitt issued orders for T.F.87 to be dissolved. Rear-Admiral Lewis left the area in the *Bayfield,* Rear-Admiral Rodgers taking command of both "Camel" and "Delta" sectors. On the 6th a strong north-easterly wind caused rough seas on the beaches and at 1800 operations over "Alpha" and "Delta" beaches had to be suspended, but were resumed next morning. On 9th September, "Alpha" beaches were closed down, and Rear-Admiral Lowry in the *Duane* withdrew from the assault area. All surplus beach personnel was moved to the ports, and the whole beach area was henceforth under the command of Rear-Admiral Rodgers. This same day Admiral Hewitt in the *Catoctin* moved to Toulon. On 16th September, the port of St. Tropez and the "Delta" beaches were closed down. On this day also in the early morning the P.T. boat patrol intercepted and pursued four explosive boats and one control boat. Hits were scored on the enemy craft, but they succeeded in escaping.

On 17th September, an American naval blimp arrived at Cuers airfield, near Toulon. R.A.F. jet-fighter pilots must have looked upon this survival from another era much as a general commanding an armoured division would have regarded one of Boadicea's war chariots, but the airship was usefully employed in accurately plotting the positions of minefields. On 25th September, "Camel" beaches were closed down and Admiral Hewitt dissolved his Task Force, sailing away from Toulon in his flagship. Rear-Admiral Davidson remained in command of the greatly reduced Support Force, and though for months afterwards convoys continued to arrive at Marseilles and Toulon with supplies for the Army, on 25th September Operation "Dragoon" came to an end.

1 H. p. 237.
2 H. p. 97, but on p. 237 it is said that 25 ships and craft were damaged.

43. Conclusion

The question of the strategic value of Operation "Dragoon", and the invasion of Southern France in relation to the Grand Strategy of the war is not for consideration in this Battle Summary. From the tactical point of view there is no doubt that Operation "Dragoon" was a resounding success. Between 15th August and 25th September a great army, consisting of 324,069 men with vehicles, was disembarked, and to maintain this force there were landed over 490,000 tons of dry stores and 325,000 barrels.[1]' All this was done with very small loss. The Seventh Army swept aside all opposition, captured Marseilles, one of the largest ports in the world, and Toulon, one of the principal naval bases in the Mediterranean, and advanced some 400 miles in 27 days to join forces with General Eisenhower on the borders of Alsace, capturing over 60,000 prisoners besides cutting off in south-western France large bodies of the enemy which eventually were obliged to surrender. The American naval casualties amounted to 35 killed, 36 missing and 243 wounded.[2] No figures are available of British and other Allied casualties but they were certainly very small. Material losses were also inconsiderable, having regard to the scope of the operation and the number of ships engaged. No major unit was sunk or badly damaged. The losses were:[3]-

Sunk:-	
British	1 M.L., 2 L.C.M.
American	1 L.S.T., 2 Y.M.S., 2 P.T., 5 L.C.V.P.
Damaged[4]*:-*	
British	1 Minesweeper, (H.M.S. Brave) 5 L.C.T., 2 M.Ls. 1 B.Y.M.S., 5 L.C.M.
American	1 Destroyer,[5] 1 Minesweeper (U.S.S. Seer), 10 L.C.I., 5 L.C.T., 1 L.C.C., 1 Y.M.S., 3 S.C., 1 P.T., 8 L.C.V.P., 1 tug, 1 salvage vessel.

By far the greater number of these casualties were caused by mines. It says much for the care and thoroughness with which the plans were drawn up that it is impossible to point to any failure in the naval organisation. It must, however, be realised that the enemy made very little resistance, and it is impossible to say what would have taken place in the transport areas and on the beaches had they been subjected to prolonged air attacks. After an operation of this nature, where there was so little opposition from the enemy, it is difficult to lay down lessons for future guidance. Admiral Hewitt in his report makes a number of recommendations,[6] but these deal mainly with matters of technical detail, and it will be sufficient to conclude by saying that a great and extremely complex operation, involving a naval force of 2,250 ships and craft, was perfectly planned and carried out with complete success.

1 H. p. 133.
2 H. p. 370.
3 H. p. 133.
4 Evidently only vessels seriously damaged are included in Admiral Hewitt's return, for several ships, including the Cactotin, were hit by bombs or shell fire.
5 U.S.S. Mackenzie was damaged by explosion during a depth charge attack on 21st August.
6 H. pp. 382-387.

APPENDIX A

SHIPS ENGAGED[1]

1. American				
WARSHIPS[2] AND AUXILIARIES				
H.Q. Ships	*Catoctin*	Vice-Admiral H.K. Hewitt		
	Duane	Rear-Admiral Lowry. Alpha Attack Force.		
	Biscayne	Rear-Admiral Rodgers. Delta Attack Force.		
Combat Loader	*Bayfield*	Rear-Admiral Lewis. Camel Attack Force.		
Cruiser	*Augusta*	Rear-Admiral Davidson. Sitka Attack Force and Reserve Gunfire Support Group.		
Battleships	*Texas*	Rear-Admiral Bryant Commanding Delta Gunfire Support Group.		
	Nevada			
	Arkansas			
Cruisers	*Tuscaloosa*	Rear-Admiral Deyo Commanding Camel Gunfire Support Group.		
	Quincy			
	Philadelphia			
	Brooklyn			
	Marblehead			
	Omaha			
	Cincinnati ?			
Aircraft Carriers	*Tulagi*	Rear-Admiral Durgin. Second-in-Command Aircraft Carrier Force.		
	Kasaan Bay			
Destroyers	*Plunkett*	Relief Fleet Flagship	*Emmons*	Des. Div. 19
			Macomb	
	Jouett	Des Div. 13	*Forrest*	Des. Div. 20
	Benson		*Fitch*	
	Niblack		*Hobson*	
	Madison	Des Div. 14	*Parker*	Des Div. 31
	Hilary P. Jones		*Kendrick*	
	C.F. Hughes		*Mackenzie*	
	Frankford	Des Div. 35	*McLanahan*	
	Carmick		*Boyle*	*Des Div. 32*
	Doyle		*Champlin*	
	McCook		*Nields*	

1 Taken in the main from Admiral Hewitt's Operation Plan at end of H., but ships known not to have been in the assault area are omitted. It is probable that some auxiliaries shown here did not in fact enter the assault area. On the other hand, the names of ships of the later follow up convoys and their escorts are not known.

2 The exact status of American Ships is sometimes difficult to ascertain. The same ship was at times a naval and at others a merchant vessel.

Destroyers	*Baldwin* *Harding* *Satterlee* *Thompson*	Des Div. 36	*Ordronaux* *Woolsey* *Ludlow* *Edison*	Des Div. 25
	Endicott	S.O. Special Operations Group	*Murphy Jeffers*	Des Div. 33
	Livermore *Eberle* *Kearney* *Ericsson*	Des Div. 21	*Butler* *Gherardi* *Herndon* *Shubrick*	Des Div. 34
	Ellyson *Hambleton* *Rodman*	Des Div. 19	*Somers* *Gleaves*	Reserve Gunfire Support Group
Destroyer Escorts[1]	*Tatum* *Haines* *Runels* *Hollis*	Cort Div. 47	*Marsh* *Currier* *F.C. Davis* *H.C. Jones*	
Combat Loaders	*Henrico* *Samuel Chase* *Anne Arundel* *Thurston* *Oberon* *Andromeda*	Alpha Assault Force	*Charles Carroll* *Thomas Jefferson* *Dorothea L. Dix* *Florence Nightingale* *Cepheus* *Achernar* *Betelgeuse*	Camel Assault Force
	Elizabeth C. Stanton *Barnett* *Joseph T. Dickman* *Lyon* *Arcturus* *Procyon*	Delta Assault Force		
Transports	*James Parker* *Marine Robin* *Santa Rosa* *General G. O. Squier*			
Destroyer (fast) Transports	*Tatnall* *Roper* *Barry* *Greene* *Osmond Ingram*			

1 Equivalent to " Hunt" Class.

Auxiliary Mine Layers	*Barricade* *Planter*	Commander Messmer, S.O. Sweeper Force		
Mine Sweepers	*Pheasant*	Min Div. 21	*Prevail*	Min Div. 16
	Raven		*Dextrous*	
	Auk		*Pioneer*	
	Broadbill		*Seer*	
	Chickadee		*Sway*	Min Div. 18
	Nuthatch		*Symbol*	
	Staff		*Strive*	Min Div. 17
	Swift		*Speed*	
	Threat		*Steady*	
	Implicit	Min Ron 11	*Sustain*	
	Incessant			
	Incredible			
	Mainstay			
	Pinnacle			
	Improve			
Salvage Vessel	*Tackle*			
Net layers	*Hackberry*			
	Pepperwood			
Repair Ships	*Vulcan*			
	Delta			
	Achelous			
Destroyer Depot Ship	*Denebola*			
Store Issue Ship	*Pleiades*			
Ammunition Ships	*Nitro*			
	Mount Baker			
Tankers	*Chemung*	*Cowanesque*		
	Winooski	*Chiwawa*		
Tugs	*Narrangansett*	*Hopi*		
	Pinto	*Edenshaw*		
	Moreno	*Evea*[1]		
	Arikara	*ATR 1*		
A.T.A.	*125, 170, 172*			
Y.T.L.	*160, 161, 165, 186, 196, 210*			

1 Shown as U.S. in H. p. 30 but wrongly as British in Annexe G. to Operation Plan.

Y.M.S.	*17, 164, 179, 250, 359, 373, 13, 18, 20, 21, 27, 34, 251, 82, 199, 355, 3, 28, 29, 37, 43, 55, 69, 83, 226, 248, 15, 24, 63, 78, 200, 303.*
S.C. (Submarine Chaser)	*524, 526, 651, 666, 690, 693, 695, 1029, 498, 535, 655, 770, 978, 979, 503, 515, 525, 530, 534, 506, 522, 532, 533, 638, 676, 691, 692, 1030, 1043.*
P.C. (Patrol Vessel)	*557, 591, 626, 1140, 1168, 1169, 1173, 1174, 1226, 1227, 545, 556, 559, 621, 1235, 1593, 1594, 1595, 1596, 542, 546, 551, 625, 627, 1597.*

P.T.[1] (Motor Torpedo Boat)	42 boats
A.S.R.C.[1] (Air Sea Rescue Craft)	16 boats
L.S.T.[2]	75 ships
L.C.I.[1]	97 craft
L.C.T.[1]	77 craft
Y.F. (Covered lighter)	*445, 447.*

MERCHANT VESSELS		
Ambrose E. Burnside	*George Handley*	*William H. Jackson*
Andrew Moore	*Lincoln Steffins*	*Edward Richardson*
James Moore	*Abel Stearns*	*George G. Meade*
John Lawson	*Albert A. Michelson*	*George Leonard*
John Trumbull	*Alexander J. Dallas*	*John B. Hood*
Josiah Bartlett	*Ethan Allen*	*James Rumsey*
Kemp P. Battle	*Turnifold M. Simmons*	*Cushing Fells*
Luther Martin	*George W. McCrary*	*Edward Burleson*
Samuel Griffin	*Henry Groves*	*Black Hawk*
William Floyd	*Connors Howell*	*Henry Ward Beecher*
William Rawle	*E. Jackson John Cropper*	*James McHenry*
John M. Morehead	*John W. Brown*	*Laura Keene*
William A. Graham	*Marion Bovard*	*Louisa M. Alcott*
Leonida Polk	*Peter J. McGuire*	*Mercy Warren*
Roger Williams	*Tabitha Brown*	*Richard Bush*
William Blount	*King S. Woolsey*	*William Moultrie*
Lucretia Mott	*William F. Cody*	*Tristam Dalton*
Tarleton Brown	*Joseph H. Nicholson*	*John S. Pillsbury*
James Jackson	*Grenville M. Dodge*	*George Bancroft*
Crosby G. Noyes	*Edwin L. Godkin*	*Bret Harte*
George Breckenbridge[3]		

1 Identification numbers not given.
2 The identification numbers of L.S.T. are not included for although given in operation plan there is nothing to show which were American-there were a few British and Greek L.S.T. engaged.
Not identified. Possibly John C. Breckinidge.

2. British

WARSHIPS		
Note. - Names of Commanding Officers when not given in reports are taken from Navy List.		
Battleship	*Ramillies*	Capt. G. B. Middleton, C.B.E., A.D.C., R.N.
Cruisers	*Orion*	Rear-Admiral J. M. Mansfield, D.S.C. Commanding Alpha Gunfire Support Group Capt. J. P. Gornall, R.N.
	Aurora	Capt. G. Barnard, C.B.E., D.S.O., R.N.
	Ajax	Capt. J. J. Weld, M.V.O., R.N..
	Black Prince	Capt. D. M. Lees, D.S.O., R.N.
	Argonaut	Capt. E. W. L. Longley-Cook, C.B.E., R.N.
	Dido	Capt. J. Terry, M.V.O., R.N.
	Sirius	Capt. R. I. M. Edwards, C.B.E., R.N.
A/A Cruisers	*Royalist*	Rear-Admiral T. H. Troubridge, D.S.O. Commanding Carrier Force Capt. J. G. Hewitt, D.S.O., R.N.
	Colombo	Capt. C. T. Jellicoe, D.S.O., D.S.C., R.N.
	Delhi	Capt. G. R. Waymouth, R.N.
	Caledon	Capt. R. F. Nichols, R.N.
Aircraft Carriers	*Khedive*	Capt. H. J. Haynes, D.S.O., D.S.C., R.N.
	Emperor	Capt. T. J. N. Hilken, D.S.O., R.N.
	Searcher	Capt. G. O. C. Davies, R.N.
	Pursuer	Capt. H. R. Graham, D.S.O., D.S.C., R.N.
	Attacker	Capt. H. B. Farncomb, D.S.O., M.V.O., R.A.N.
	Stalker	Capt. H. S. Murray-Smith, R.N.
	Hunter	Capt. H. H. McWilliam, R.N.
Destroyers	*Troubridge*	Capt. C. L. Firth, R.N., D.24.
	Tuscan	Lt. Cdr. E. N. Wood, R.N.V.R.
	Tyrian	Cdr. R. H. Mills, D.S.O., D.S.C., R.N.
	Teazer	Lt. Cdr. R. A. F. Talbot, D.S.O., R.N.
	Tumult	Lt. Cdr. N. Lanyon, D.S.C., R.N.
	Tenacious	Lt. Cdr. D. F. Townsend, R.N.
	Terpsichore	Cdr. A. C. Behague, O.B.E., D.S.C., R.N.
	Termagant	Lt. Cdr. J. P. Scatchard, D.S.C., R.N.
	Lookout	Lt. Cdr. D. H. F. Hetherington, R.N.
	Aldenham	Cdr. J. G. Farrant, R.N., D.5.
	Beaufort	Lt. J. R. Moore, D.S.C., R.N.
	Belvoir	Lt. W. D. Shaw, R.N.
	Whaddon	Lt. Cdr. R. L. Green, R.N.V.R.
	Blackmore	Lt. J. S. Kerans, R.N.
	Eggesford	Lt. G. H. Evans, R.N.
	Lauderdale	Lt. R. L. Boddy, R.N.

Destroyers	*Farndale*	Lt. Cdr. H. E. F. Tweedie, D.S.C., R.N., D.18
	Atherstone	Lt. E. I. Pilditch, R.N.
	Brecon	Lt. N. R. H. Rodney, R.N.
	Calpe	Lt. Cdr. N. F. R. Gill, R.N.R.
	Catterick	Lt. D. P. William, D.S.C., R.N.
	Cleveland	Lt. J. C. Lapage, R.N.
	Haydon	Lt. R. G. R. Clay, R.N.
	Bicester	Lt. Cdr. R. W. F. Northcott, D.S.O., R.N.
	Liddesdale	Lt. C. J. Bateman, R.N.
	Oakley	Lt. G. R. P. Gooden, R.N.
	Zetland	Lt. C. R. Bax, R.N.
L.S.I.	*Keren*[1]	Cdr. S. E. Crewe-Read, R.N.
	Prince Henry	Capt. V. S. Godfrey, R.C.N.
	Prince David	Cdr. T. D. Kelly, R.C.N.R.
	Princess Beatrix	Lt. Cdr. J. D. King, R.N.R.
	Prince Albert	Lt. Cdr. H. B. Peate, R.D., R.N.R.
	Prince Baudouin	Lt. Cdr. W. E. Gelling, D.S.C., R.D., R.N.R.
L.S.T. (Killer)	*Bruiser*	Lt. Cdr. J. Stretch, R.N.R.,
	Thruster	Lt. Cdr. W. W. McMullan, D.S.C., R.N.R.
Minesweeping Depot Ship	*Product*	Lt. Cdr. B. P. A. Wing, D.S.C., R.N.R.
Minesweepers	*Rothesay*	Cdr. A. A. Martin, D.S.C., R.D., R.N.R., M/S 13
	Bude	Lt. E. A. C. Phillips, D.S.C., R.N.R.
	Brixham	Lt. W. K. Lewis, R.N.V.R.
	Polruan	Lt. Cdr. C. D. Sampson, D.S.C., R.N.V.R.
	Aries	Lt. Cdr. C. R. Fraser, R.N.V.R.
	Stornoway	Lt. J. E. Freeth, R.N.V.R.
	Rhyl	Lt. Cdr. N. E. Morley, D.S.C., R.N.V.R.
	Rinaldo	Cdr. C. H. Corbet-Singleton, D.S.C., R.N., M/S 19
	Antares	Lt. Cdr. A. H. Diack, R.N.
	Arcturus	Lt. C. M. Partridge, R.N.
	Brave	Lt. Cdr. F. S. Tolliday, R.N.R.
	Spanker	Lt. Cdr. I. B. Moffatt, R.D., R.N.R.
	Rosario	Lt. Cdr. F. E. Brooking, R.N.
	Larne	Cdr. H. L. Jenkins, R.N., M/S 5
	Clinton	Lt. K. A. Gadd, D.S.C., R.N.R.
	Octavia	Lt. Cdr. L. C. D. Godwin, D.S.C., R.N.
	Stormcloud	Lt. Cdr. M. L. M. Trevor, R.N.V.R.
	Welfare	Lt. Cdr. J. A. Pearson, D.S.C., R.N.R.

1 Unlike the Americans, whose combat loaders and transports are naval vessels, many British L.S.I. and all transports are merchant ships under which heading they will be found, This also applies to repair ships and other types of auxiliaries,

Danlayers	*Nebb*	Lt. H. G. Davies, R.N.V.R.
	Foula	Lt. Cdr. E. R. O. Greenstreet, R.N.V.R.
	Borealis	Lt. H. P. Griffiths, R.N.V.R..
	Kintyre	Lt. Cdr. P. A. Tritton, R.N.V.R.
	Satsa	Lt. H. Olsberg, R.N.V.R.
	Calm	Lt. K. Gibson, R.N.V.R.
M/S Trawlers	*Crowlin*	Skpr. Lt. A. Smith, R.N.R.
	Ailsa Craig	Lt. T. G. Hornsby, R.N.R.
	Mewstone	Skpr. Lt. J. Mawey, R.N.R.
	Skokolm	Lt. B. M. Brabant, R.N.V.R.
Gunboats	*Aphis*	Lt. E. E. Clifton, R.N.R.
	Scarab	Lt. E. A. Hawkesworth, R.N.V.R.
Corvettes	*Aubretia*	Lt. Cdr. G. D. Fowler, R.N.R.
	Columbine	Lt. J. C. Grose, R.N.R.
Fighter Defence Ships	*Stuart Prince*	Cdr. W. A. Moens, R.N.
	Ulster Queen	Capt. M. H. J. Bennett, R.D., R.N.R.
Air Sea Rescue Ship	*Antwerp*	Lt. Cdr. F. R. Rand, R.N.
L.S.D.	*Highway*	Lt. Cdr. R. A. Vallings, D.S.C., R.N.R.
	Eastway	Lt. Cdr. W. A. Fletcher, R.N.R.
Boom Vessels	*Barholm*	Lt. C. L. R. Turnor, R.N.V.R.
	Barford	Boom Skpr. R. N. Mecklenburgh, R.N.R.
	Barmond	Lt. J. B. Gibson, R.N.R.
	Bardolf	Lt. J. H. Briggs, R.N.R.
Tugs	*Aspirant*	*Charon*
	Empire Spitfire	*Mindful*
	Empire Anne	*Vagrant*
	Athlete	
B.Y.M.S.	*2009, 2022, 2026, 2027, 2171, 2172*	
M.L.	*299, 337, 581, 451, 456, 461, 478, 576, 121, 338, 462, 554, 563, 565, 559, 560, 562, 567, 555, 556, 557, 564, 273, 336, 458, 463, 469, 471.*	
M.F.V.	*47, 68, 90, 105, 129, 132* (Manned by French crews)	
Air Sea Rescue Craft	1 boat (Included for the sake of completeness but in reality R.A.F. not naval)	
Balloon Tender	*F.T.6. F.T.30*	
L.S.E.	1 ship	
L.S.F. (F.D.T.)	13	
L.C.F.	*4, 8, 10, 14, 16, 17*	
L.C.G.	*4, 8, 12, 14, 20*	

L.S.T.	1 ship (Bruiser and Thruster already listed)
L.C.I.	27 craft
L.C.T.	65 craft
L.C.T.(R)	30 craft (14 manned by American crews).

AUXILIARIES AND MERCHANT VESSELS

L.S.I.	*Derbyshire*	*Circassia*
	Dunera	*Winchester Castle*
	Dilwara	
L.S.P.	*Ascania*	
L.S.G.	*Ennerdale*	
	Dewdale	
L.S.C.	*Empire Elaine*	
Transports	*Cameronian*	*Durban Castle*
	Staffordshire	*Worcestershire*
Water Carriers	*Empire Harp*	*Myriel*
	Empire Fawn	*Po*[1]
Refrigerator Ship	*Hebe II.*	
Tankers	*Celerol*	*Nasprite*
	Empire Gawain	*Empire Lass*
	Spindletop	*Empire Fay*
	Cotton Valley	*Empire Damsel*
Collier	*Cara*	
Ammunition Ships	*Empire Spinney*	*Procris*
	Empire Gat	*Fendris*

Cargo Ships	*Samwash*	*Ocean Gallant*	*Ocean Pride*
	Empire Pride	*Samoa*	*Chertsey*
	Eastern Prince	*Sampan*	*Samsteel*
	Takliwa	*Empire Clarion*	*Fort Gaspereau*
	Sambre	*Harlesden*	*Fort Richelieu*
	Fort Marin	*Empire Outpost*	*Fort Grahame*
	Fort Chesterfield	*Jersey Hart*	*Fort Aklavik*
	Fort Frontenac	*Ocean Traveller*	*Essex Trader*
	Fort Beausejour	*Ocean Glory*	*Coulgorm*
	Fort Cumberland	*Ocean Vesper*	*Ocean Rider*
	Empire Rosalind	*Fort Michipicoten*	*Fort Pembina*
	Empire Noble	*Fort Frobisher*	*Fort Maisonneuve*
	Empire Unicorn	*Thistlemuir*	*Ocean Gipsy*
	Norman Monarch	*Thistledale*	*Fort Stager*
	Ocean Messenger		

1 Given in Operation Plan but cannot be identified.

3. French			
WARSHIPS			
Battleship	*Lorraine*		
Cruisers	*Georges Leygues*	Rear-Admiral Jaujard	*Duguay Trouin*
	Gloire		*Emile Bertin*
	Montcalm		*Jeanne D'Arc*
Destroyers	*Fortune*		*Le Fantasque*
	Forbin		*Le Malin*
	Simoun		*Le Terrible*
	Tempête		*L'Alcyon*
Escorteurs (Equivalent to HUNT Class)	*Hova*		
	Algerien		
	Somali		
	Marocain		
	Tunisien		
Sloops	*Commandant Domine*		*Commandant Bory*
	La Moqueuse		*Commandant Delage*
	La La Gracieuse		*La Boudeuse*
Y.M.S.	*271*		
Chasseurs	*90, 95*		
Ammunition Ships	*Quercy*	Tankers	*Le Mekong*
	Barfleur		*Elorn*
			Var

4. Greek	
WARSHIPS	
Destroyers	*Navarinon*
	Pindos
	Crete
	Themistocles
L.S.T.	*3 ships*

5. Polish	
MERCHANT VESSELS	
L.S.I.	*Sobieski*
Transport	*Batory*

6. Dutch	
MERCHANT VESSELS	
Collier	*Amstel*
Cargo Ships	*Van der Capelle*
	Jan Lievens
	Volendam
7. Norwegian	
MERCHANT VESSELS	
Tanker	*Elise*
Cargo Ships	*President le Vogue*
	Falkefjell
8. Belgian	
MERCHANT VESSELS	
Tanker	*Alexandre Andre*
9. Italian	
MERCHANT VESSELS	
Tanker	*Tarvisio*

APPENDIX B

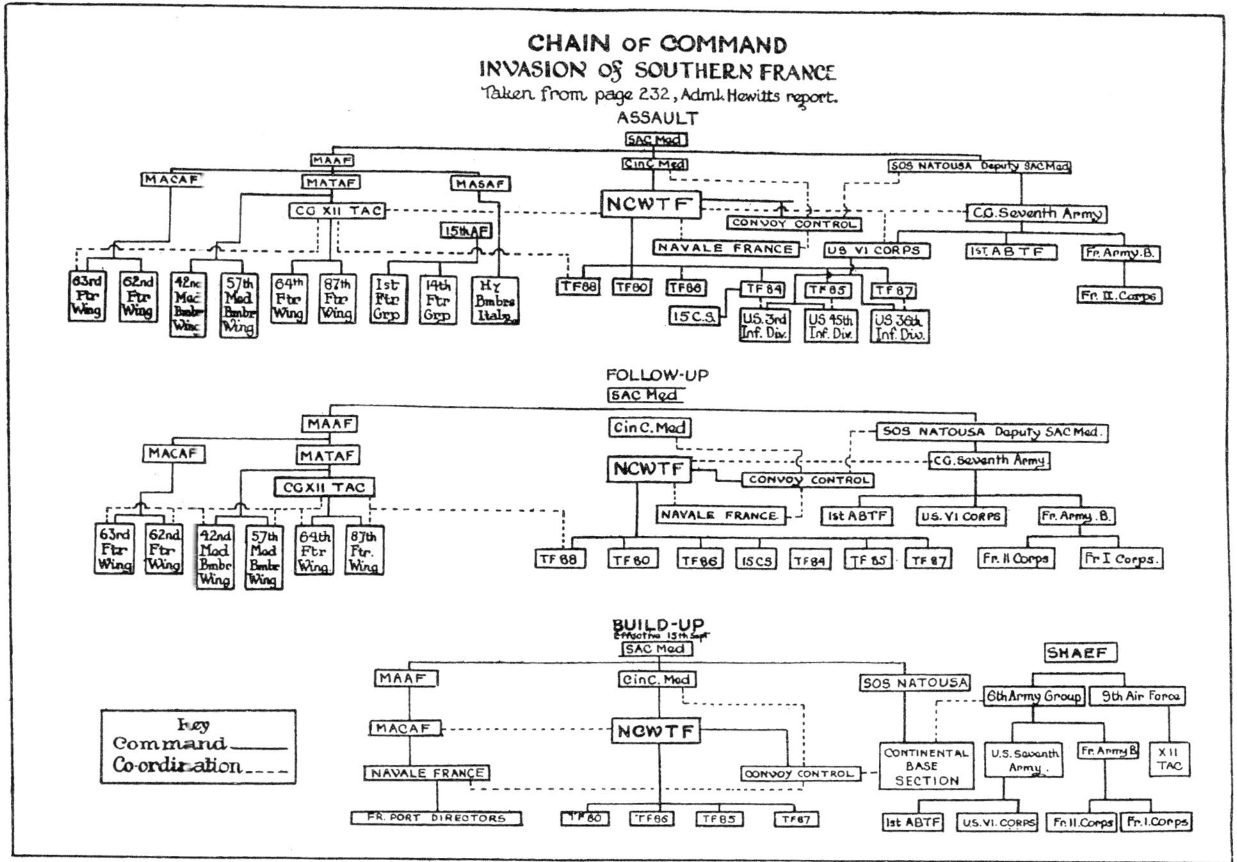

CHAIN OF COMMAND
INVASION OF SOUTHERN FRANCE
Taken from page 232, Adml. Hewitts report.
ASSAULT
SAC Med
MAAF
CinC Med
SOS NATOUSA Deputy SAC Med
MACAF
MATAF
MASAF
NCWTF
CG XII TAC
15th AF
CONVOY CONTROL
C.G. Seventh Army
NAVALE FRANCE
US VI CORPS
1st A B T F
Fr. Army. B.
63rd Ftr Wing
62nd Ftr Wing
42nd Med Bmbr Wing
57th Med Bmbr Wing
64th Ftr Wing
87th Ftr Wing
1st Ftr Grp
14th Ftr Grp
Hy Bmbrs Italy
TF 88
TF 80
TF 86
TF 84
TF 85
TF 87
15 C.S.
US. 3rd Inf. Div.
US 45th Inf. Div.
US 36th Inf. Div.
Fr. II. Corps
FOLLOW-UP
SAC Med
MAAF
Cin C. Med
SOS NATOUSA Deputy SAC Med.
MACAF
MATAF
NCWTF
C.G. Seventh Army
CG XII TAC
CONVOY CONTROL
NAVALE FRANCE
1st ABTF
US. VI CORPS
Fr. Army. B.
63rd Ftr Wing
62nd Ftr Wing
42nd Med Bmbr Wing
57th Med Bmbr Wing
64th Ftr Wing
87th Ftr. Wing
TF 88
TF 80
TF 86
15 CS
TF 84
TF 85
TF 87
Fr. II Corps
Fr I Corps.
BUILD-UP
Effective 15th Sept
SAC Med
SHAEF
MAAF
Cin C. Med
SOS NATOUSA
6th Army Group
9th Air Force
Key
Command
Co-ordination
MACAF
NCWTF
NAVALE FRANCE
CONVOY CONTROL
CONTINENTAL BASE SECTION
U.S. Seventh Army.
Fr. Army B
XII TAC
FR. PORT DIRECTORS
TF 80
TF 86
TF 85
TF 87
1st ABTF
US. VI. CORPS
Fr. II. Corps
Fr. I. Corps
TSD/HS (409).

APPENDIX C

'S' CONVOYS AND GUNFIRE SUPPORT GROUPS

"S" Convoys

S.F.1. (CAMEL)		S.F.1A (DELTA)	
CONVOY	ESCORT	CONVOY	ESCORT
Bayfield	*Satterlee*	*Ascania*	*Baldwin*
Keren	*H.P. Jones*	*Dilwara*	*Madison*
Squier	*C.F. Hughes*	*Marine Robin*	*Carmick*
Carrol	*Thompson*	*Santa Rosa*	*Marsh*
Jefferson	*McCook*	*Barnett*	*Haines*
Dix		*Dickman*	
Nightingale		*Stanton*	
Cepheus		*Lyon*	
Achernar		*Arcturus*	
Betelgeuse		*Procyon*	
Eastway			

S.F.1B. (ALPHA)			
CONVOY	ESCORT	CONVOY	ESCORT
Catoctin	*Frankford*	*Anne Arundel*	
Plunkett	*Benson*	*Thurston*	*Lorraine*
Dunera	*Runels*	*Oberon*	
Derbyshire	*Hollis*	*Andromeda*	
Henrico	*P.C. 591*	*Highway*	
Chase			

Convoys S.F.1, 1A and 1B sail from Naples August 13th, Convoy Route I, Speed 12 knots. E.T.A. at position AN, (SFI), AM, (SFIA), and position AL, (SFIB) at 2000/August 14th.

S.Y.1.		
Prince Henry	*Tatnall*	*Roper*
Prince David	*Barry*	*Osmond Ingram*
Princess Beatrix	*Greene*	*Themistocles*
Prince Albert		
Prince Baudouin		

Sail from Naples August 11th. Convoy Routes 1 and 10. Speed 14 kts. Stage at Propriano. Sail August 14th. E.T.A. position CB, 2120 August 14th. Sweepers and M.L.'s rendezvous at position CB. P.T.'s from Calvi rendezvous at position CB.

<table>
<tr><th colspan="3">Gunfire Support Groups</th></tr>
<tr><td colspan="3">CAMEL</td></tr>
<tr><td>Arkansas
Tuscaloosa
Brooklyn
Marblehead
Argonaut
Duguay Trouin
Emile Bertin</td><td>Parker
McKenzie
Kendrick
McLanahan
Boyle
Champlin</td><td>Ordronaux
Nields
Woolsey
Ludlow
Edison</td></tr>
<tr><td colspan="3">Sail from Palermo August 12th. Convoy Route 6. Rendezvous with S.F.1, 1600/August 14th.</td></tr>
<tr><td colspan="3">DELTA</td></tr>
<tr><td>Texas
Nevada
Philadelphia
George Leygues
Montcalm</td><td>Le Fantasque
Le Terrible
Le Malin</td><td>Ellyson
Hambleton
Rodman
Emmons
Macomb
Forrest Fitch
Hobson</td></tr>
<tr><td colspan="3">Sail from Taranto, August 11th. Convoy Route 2. Rendezvous with S.F.1A, 1800/August 14th.</td></tr>
<tr><td colspan="3">ALPHA</td></tr>
<tr><td>Ramillies
Orion
Aurora
Ajax
Black Prince</td><td>Quincy
Gloire
Livermore
Eberle</td><td>Kearney
Ericsson
Termagant
Terpsichore</td></tr>
<tr><td colspan="3">Sailed from Malta August 11th. Convoy Route 2. Owing to late arrival from U.K., Ramillies sailed from Algiers direct for assault area. Rendezvous with Alpha G.S.G. 0500/ Aug. 15th.</td></tr>
</table>

<table>
<tr><td colspan="5">SITKA</td></tr>
<tr><td>Augusta</td><td>Dido</td><td>Lookout</td><td>Gleaves</td><td>Somers</td></tr>
<tr><td colspan="5">Sail from Naples August 12th. Convoy Routes 1 and 10. Rendezvous with S.Y.1 at 2120/ August 14th.</td></tr>
</table>

<table>
<tr><th colspan="4">"S" Convoys</th></tr>
<tr><td colspan="2">S.F.2 (CAMEL)</td><td colspan="2">S.F.2A (DELTA)</td></tr>
<tr><td>CONVOY</td><td>ESCORT</td><td>CONVOY</td><td>ESCORT</td></tr>
<tr><td>Antwerp
30 L.C.I.</td><td>Niblack
Product
Speed
Strive
Sustain
Steady
1 P.C.
2 S.C.</td><td>38 L.C.I.</td><td>Crete
Currier
Rinaldo
Antares
Arcturus
Spanker
Rosario
Brave
5 P.C.</td></tr>
<tr><td colspan="4">S.F.2B. (ALPHA)</td></tr>
<tr><td colspan="2">CONVOY</td><td colspan="2">ESCORT</td></tr>
<tr><td colspan="2">Ulster Queen
47 L.C.I.</td><td colspan="2">Oakley
4 P.C.
4 S.C.</td></tr>
<tr><td colspan="4">Convoys S.F.2, 2A and 2B sail from Naples August 12th. Convoy Route 1. Speed 11 knots. Stage at Ajaccio August 13th. Sail 1700/August 14th. E.T.A. at position AN (S.F.2), position AM (S.F.2A), and position AL (S.F.2B), 2300/August 14th. Antwerp to leave convoy in Straits of Bonifacio and proceed to Bastia.</td></tr>
<tr><td colspan="2">S.M.1 (CAMEL)</td><td colspan="2">S.M.1A (DELTA)</td></tr>
<tr><td>CONVOY</td><td>ESCORT</td><td>CONVOY</td><td>ESCORT</td></tr>
<tr><td>Dewdale
Elise
Elorn
Var
Empire Damsel
Empire Fawn
Y.T.L. 210
24 L.S.T.</td><td>Bicester
Crowlin
Ailsa Craig
Mewstone
Stokkolm
3 P.C.
3 S.C.</td><td>Biscayne
Ennerdale
Narraganset
Planter
Pinto
L.S.F. 13
Empire Fay
23 L.S.T.</td><td>Liddesdale
Sway
Symbol
5 Y.M.S.
4 P.C.
A.T.A. 125</td></tr>
<tr><td colspan="4">S.M.1B (ALPHA)</td></tr>
<tr><td colspan="2">CONVOY</td><td colspan="2">ESCORT</td></tr>
<tr><td>Empire Elaine
Barricade
Empire Gawain
Achelous</td><td>Myriel
Hopi
A.T.R. 1.
22 L.S.T.</td><td>Prevail
Dextrous
Pioneer
Seer</td><td>2 P.C.
5 S.C.
5 Y.M.S.</td></tr>
<tr><td colspan="4">Convoys S.M.1, lA and 1B sail from Naples, August 12th. Convoy Route 1. Speed 8 knots. E.T.A. at A.N. (S.M.1), A.M. (S.M.1A) and A.L. (S.M.1B), 1700/August 14th. Empire Fawn, Myriel, Var and Achelous to detach from convoy off Ajaccio, and proceed to that port to join later convoys or to await orders. Empire Fay and Empire Damsel sail from Maddalena and join convoy off that port. Empire Gawain to join convoy off Maddalena and detach from convoy off Ajaccio.</td></tr>
</table>

S.S.I. (CAMEL)		
CONVOY		ESCORT
Foula	*Stuart Prince*	*Zetland*
Arikara	40 L.C.T.	5 S.C.
Mindful	2 L.C.F.	6 Y.M.S.
Vagrant	1 L.C.G.	6 B.Y.M.S.
Moreno	14 L.C.T. (R)	2 P.C.
Po	A.T.A. *172*	6 M.L.
Bardolf	2 M.F.V.	
Spindletop		

S.S.1A (DELTA)		
CONVOY		ESCORT
Cara	42 L.C.T.	*Tatum*
Aspirant	2 L.C.F.	5 S.C.
Charon	2 L.C.G.	5 Y.M.S.
Athlete	6 L.C.T. (R)	8 M.L.
Barford	1 Balloon Tender	
Barmond	Y.T.L. *186*	
Satsa	Y.T.L. *196*	
Calm	2 M.F.V.	

S.S.1B (ALPHA)			
CONVOY		ESCORT	
Duane	2 M.F.V.	*F. C. Davis*	*Clinton*
Empire Lass	A.T.A. *170*	*Rothesay*	*Octavia*
Nebb	1 L.S.T.	*Bude*	*Stormcloud*
Borealis	42 L.C.T.	*Brixham*	*Welfare*
Kintyre	2 L.C.F.	*Polruan*	3 P.C.
Barholm	2 L.C.G.	*Rhyl*	9 S.C.
Empire Anne	10 L.C.T. (R)	*Stornoway*	5 Y.M.S.
Empire Spitfire	1 Ballon tender	*Larne*	Y.T.L. *165*
Arnstel	(L.C.T.)		
Evea			

Convoys S.S.1, 1A and 1B sail from Naples August 9th. Convoy Route 1. Speed 5½ knots. Stage at Ajaccio. Sail August 13th. E.T.A. at A.N. (S.S.I), A.M. (S.S.I.A.), and A.L. (S.S.I.B.), 1100/August 14th. The six M.F.V.'s were to sail from Ajaccio, and join convoy at 0300/August 14th. *Spindletop* to join convoy off Maddalena and leave at Ajaccio. *Empire Lass* to join convoy off Maddalena. *Amstel* and *Po* remain at Ajaccio. *Cara* to detach off Maddalena, to proceed to that port. *Larne, Clinton, Octavia, Stormcloud, Welfare, Kintyre,* and also 4 M.L's from S.S.1A, rendezvous with convoy S.Y.I. at 2120/ August 14th. The six M.L's in S.S.I, join off Maddalena. *Stuart Prince* leaves convoy at Ajaccio, and joins Diversion Group.

APPENDIX D
CONVOYS

<table>
<tr><th colspan="2">Special Convoy No. 2</th></tr>
<tr><td>CONVOY</td><td>ESCORT</td></tr>
<tr><td>Winchester Castle, Bruiser
James Parker, Thruster</td><td>Harding
Doyle</td></tr>
<tr><td colspan="2">Sail from Oran, August 11th. Convoy Route 3. Speed 12 knots. E.T.A. position A.L., 0800/August 15th. E.T.A. Assault Area, 1600/August 15th.</td></tr>
</table>

<table>
<tr><th colspan="4">A.M.1</th></tr>
<tr><td colspan="4">CONVOY</td></tr>
<tr><td>Bret Harte
Edwin L. Godkin
Crosby S. Noyes
George Bancroft
George Breckenbridge</td><td>Grenville M. Dodge
James Jackson
John S. Pillsbury
Joseph H. Nicholson
Tarleton Brown</td><td>Tristram Dalton
William F. Cody
Lucretia Mott
William Moultree
King S. Woolsey</td><td>Empire Gat
Empire Spinney
Fendris
Procris
Denebola
4 L.S.T.</td></tr>
<tr><td colspan="4">ESCORT</td></tr>
<tr><td>Catterick
Cleveland</td><td colspan="2">Calpe
Staff</td><td>Swift
Threat</td></tr>
<tr><td colspan="4">Sail from Oran August 10th., Convoy Route 3, Speed 7½ kts. E.T.A. position AM, 0530/August 15th. E.T.A. Assault Area, 1800/August 15th. Denebola to detach off Cagliari. Empire Gat, Empire Spinney, Fendris and Procris to detach off Propriano.</td></tr>
</table>

<table>
<tr><th colspan="4">S.M.2</th></tr>
<tr><td colspan="4">CONVOY</td></tr>
<tr><td>Ambrose E. Burnside
Andrew Moore
James Moore
John Lawson
John Trumbull
Josiah Bartlett
Kemp P. Battle
Luther Martin
Samuel Griffin
William Floyd
William Rawle

John M. Morehead
William A. Graham</td><td>Samwash
Jan Lievens
Leonida Polk
Roger Williams
George Handley
Lincoln Steffins
Abel Stearns
Albert A. Michelson
Alexander J. Dallas
Ethan Allen
Furnifold M. Simmons
George W. McCrary
Henry Groves Connors</td><td>Howell E. Jackson
John Cropper
John W. Brown
Marion Bovard
Peter J. McGuire
Tabitha Brown
William H. Jackson
Edward Richardson
Celerol
George G. Meade
George Leonard

John B. Hood
James Rumsey</td><td>Black Hawk
Cushing Eells
Edward Burleson
Henry Ward Beecher
James McHenry
Laura Keene
Louisa M. Alcott
Mercy Warren
Richard Rush
William Blount
Le Mekong

Edenshaw
Empire Harp</td></tr>
</table>

ESCORT			
Aldenham	*Beaufort*	*Belvoir*	*Whadden*
Blackmore	*Eggesford*	*Pindos*	*Lauderdale*

Sail from Naples August 13th. Convoy Route 1, Speed 9 knots, E.T.A. position A.L. 0630/August 15th. E.T.A. Assault Area, 1600/August 15th. *Celerol* to join convoy off Maddalena *Le Mekong* to detach from convoy and proceed to Ajaccio.

T.M.1

CONVOY			
Sambre	*Ocean Pride*	*Empire Rosalind*	*Thistlemuir*
Fort Marin	*Chertsey*	*Empire Noble*	*Thistledale*
Fort Chesterfield	*Samsteel*	*Empire Unicorn*	*Van der Capelle*
Ocean Gallant	*Fort Gaspereau*	*Norman Monarch*	*Essex Trader*
Samoa	*Fort Richelieu*	*Ocean Messenger*	*Coulgorm*
Sampan	*Fort Graham*	*Ocean Traveller*	*Ocean Rider*
Empire Clarion	*Fort Aklavik*	*Ocean Glory*	*Fort Pembina*
Harlesden	*Fort Frontenac*	*Ocean Vesper*	*Fort Maisonneuve*
Empire Outpost	*Fort Beausejour*	*Fort Michipicoten*	*Ocean Gypsy*
Jersey Hart	*Fort Cumberland*	*Fort Frobisher*	*Fort Stager*

ESCORT		
Tempête	*La Moqueuse*	*Commandant Bory*
Alcyon	*La Gracieuse*	*Commandant Domine*
Somali	*La Boudeuse*	*Aubretia*
Tunisien	*Commandant-Delage*	*Columbine*
Farndale		

Sail from Taranto, August 10th. Convoy Route 2. Speed 7½ kts. E.T.A. position A.L. 0130/August 16th. E.T.A. Assault Area, 1410/August 16th.

T.F.1

CONVOY		ESCORT
Circassia	*Empire Pride*	*Forbin*
Sobieski	*Eastern Prince*	*Fortune*
Batory	*Takliwa*	*Simoun*
Cameronian	*Volendam*	*Hova*
Staffordshire	*Worcestershire*	*Algerien*
Durban Castle		*Marocain*
		H.C. Jones

Sail from Taranto on August 12th, Convoy Route 2, Speed 12 kts E.T.A. position A.L., 1000/August 16th. E.A.T. Assault Area, 1800/August 16th

<table>
<tr><th colspan="4">CARRIER FORCE</th></tr>
<tr><td>Royalist
Delhi
Khedive
Emperor
Searcher
Pursuer
Attacker</td><td>Caledon
Colombo
Tulagi
Kasaan Bay
Stalker
Hunter</td><td>Troubridge
Tuscan
Tumult
Tenacious
Tyrian
Teazer
Navarinon</td><td>Murphy
Jeffers
Butler
Gherardi
Herndon
Shubrick</td></tr>
<tr><td colspan="4">Sail from Malta, August 12th. Tunisian War Channel and Convoy Route 2.</td></tr>
</table>

<table>
<tr><th colspan="2">SPECIAL NO. 1</th></tr>
<tr><td>CONVOY</td><td>ESCORT</td></tr>
<tr><td>President le Vogue
Falkefjell
Tarvisio</td><td>2 P.C's.</td></tr>
<tr><td colspan="2">Sail in shuttle from Palermo to Ajaccio, commencing Palermo, August 14th.</td></tr>
</table>

<table>
<tr><th colspan="3">DIVERSION GROUP</th></tr>
<tr><td>Endicott
Aphis
Scarab</td><td>Antwerp
Stuart Prince</td><td>17 A.S.R.C.
8 P.T.
8 M.L.</td></tr>
<tr><td colspan="3">Diversion Forces sail from Ajaccio, Calvi, and Bastia, August 14th.</td></tr>
</table>

INDEX

The entries refer to sections, not to pages. The nationality of L.S.T., L.C.I. and L.C.T. is generally unknown.

PLAN 1

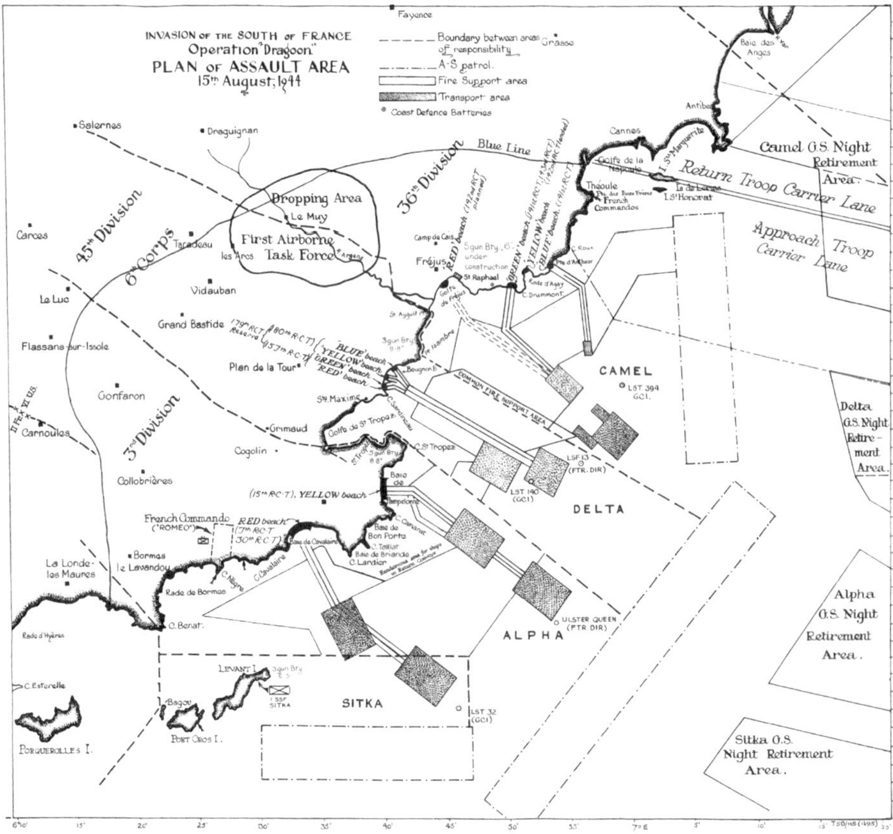
INVASION of the SOUTH of FRANCE
Operation "Dragoon"
PLAN of ASSAULT AREA
15th August, 1944
Boundary between areas of responsibility
A-S patrol.
Fire Support area
Transport area
Coast Defence Batteries
Blue Line
Dropping Area
First Airborne Task Force
45th Division
6th Corps
36th Division
3rd Division
Return Troop Carrier Lane
Approach Troop Carrier Lane
Camel G.S. Night Retirement Area.
Delta G.S. Night Retire-ment Area.
Alpha G.S. Night Retirement Area.
Sitka G.S. Night Retirement Area.
CAMEL
DELTA
ALPHA
SITKA
COMMON FIRE SUPPORT AREA
Cannes
Antibes
Grasse
Fayence
Draguignan
Salernes
Le Muy
Taradeau
les Arcs
Fréjus
St Raphael
Vidauban
Le Luc
Carces
Flassans-sur-Issole
Grand Bastide
Plan de la Tour
Gonfaron
Carnoules
Grimaud
Cogolin
St. Maxime
Golfe de St Tropez
C. St Tropez
Collobrières
Bormes
le Lavandou
La Londe-les Maures
Rade de Bormes
C. Benat
Rade d'Hyères
C. Esterelle
Porquerolles I.
Port Cros I.
Levant I.
Bagou
Théoule
French Commandos
French Commando ("ROMEO")
RED beach (7th R.C.T. 30th R.C.T.)
(15th R.C.T.) YELLOW beach
LST 394 GCI.
LSF 13 (FTR. DIR)
LST 140 (GCI)
ULSTER QUEEN (FTR DIR)
LST 32 (GCI)
I. Ste Marguerite
I. St Honorat
Golfe de la Napoule
Baie des Anges
Baie de Cavalaire
Baie de Bon Porto
C. Camarat
C. Lardier
Baie de Briande

DRAGOON PLAN 2

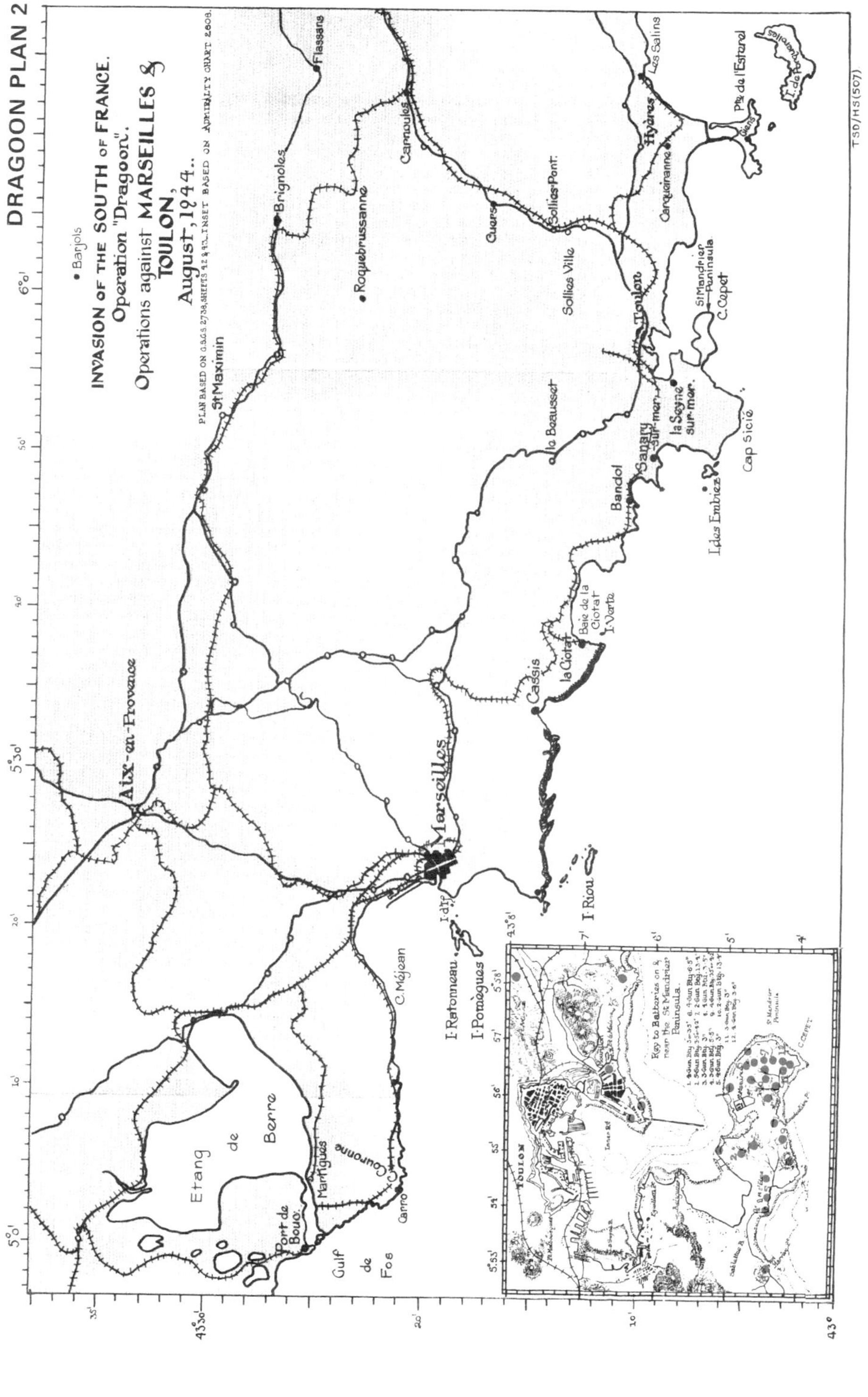

DRAGOON PLAN 3

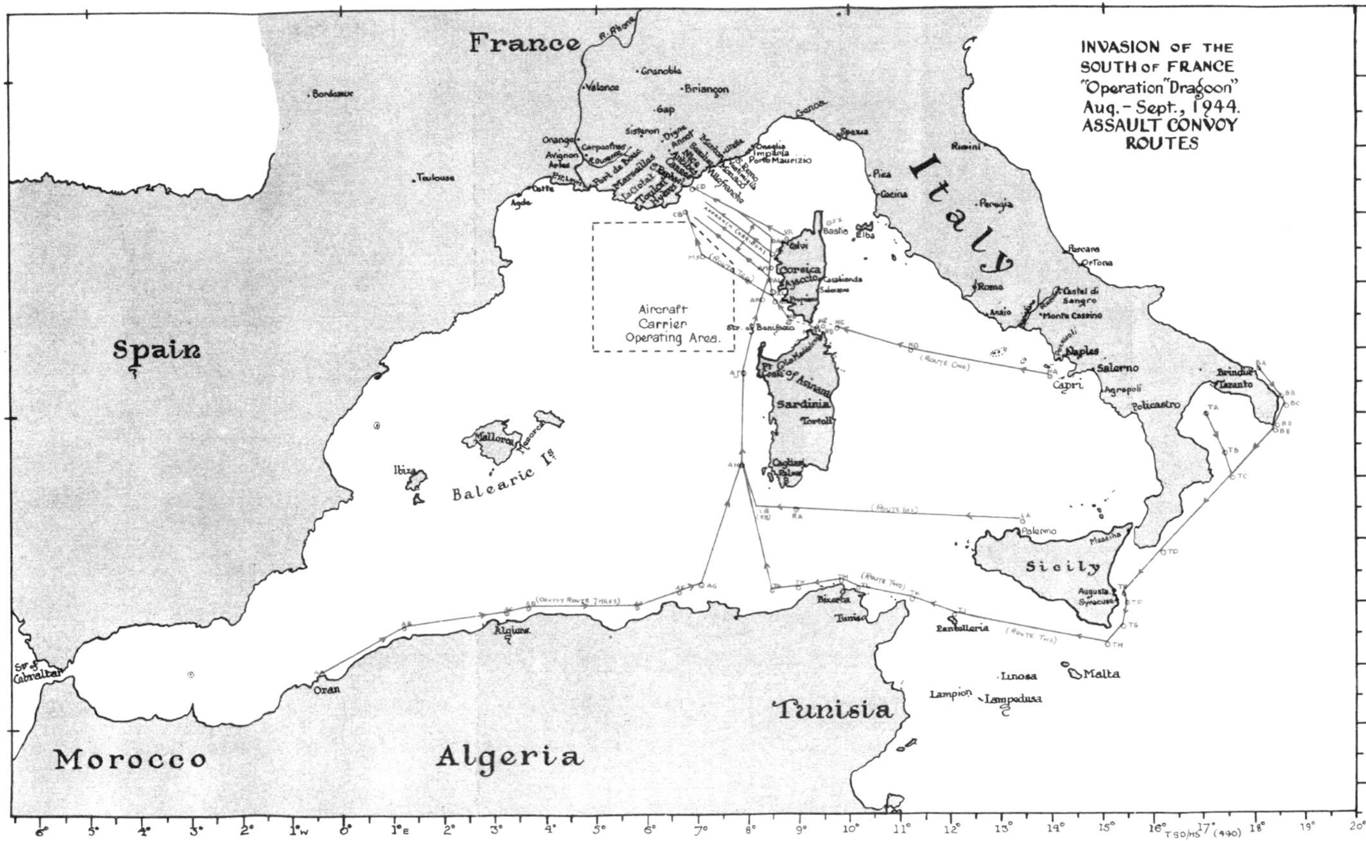

DRAGOON PLAN 4

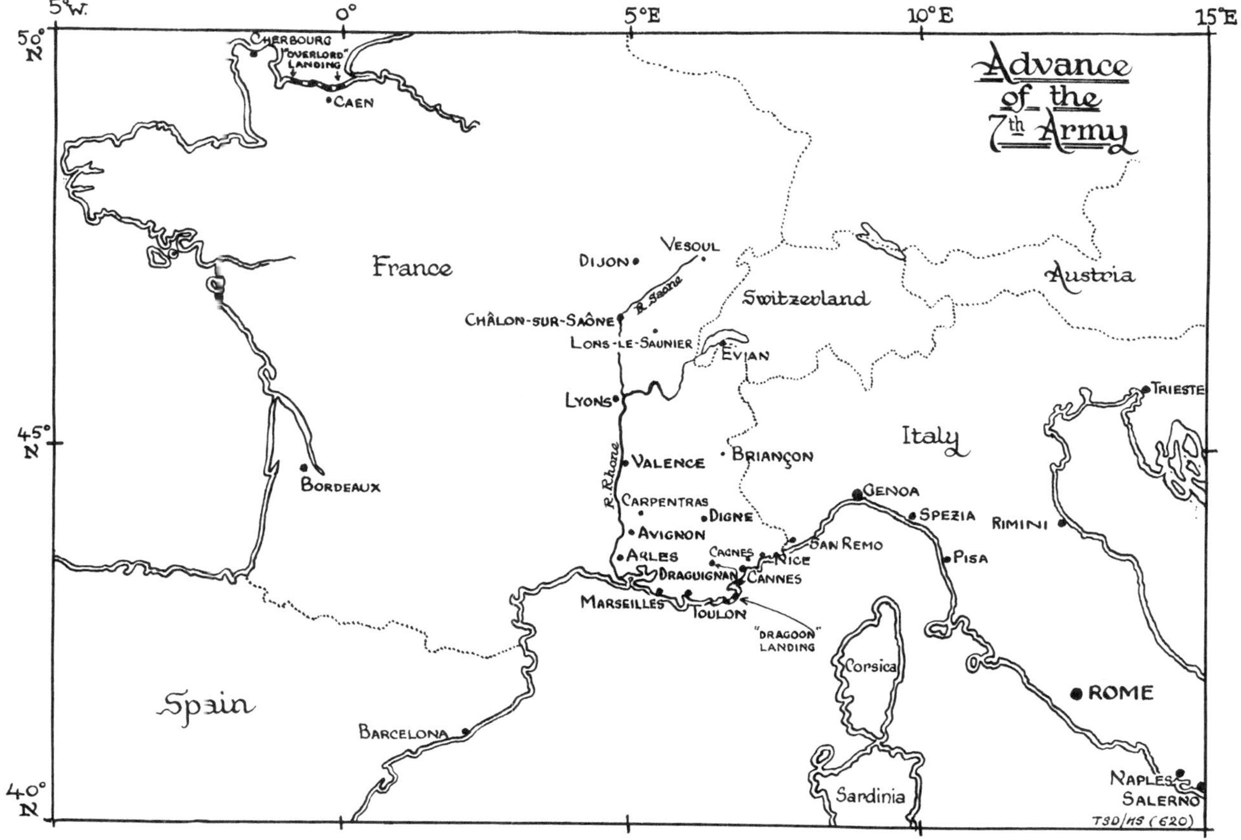